SHAW, LEDROIT PARK & BLOOMINGDALE

— IN —

WASHINGTON, D.C.

An Oral History

SHILPI MALINOWSKI

THE
History
PRESS

Published by The History Press
Charleston, SC
www.historypress.com

Copyright © 2021 by Shilpi Malinowski
All rights reserved

First published 2021

ISBN 9781467149693

Library of Congress Control Number: 2021943560

To my sons, Hugo and Leo.

CONTENTS

PREFACE

I n 2019, I quietly entered living rooms across the most gentrified neighborhood in Washington, D.C., and I listened.

By some measures, the 20001 zip code encompasses the most gentrified neighborhood in the country. The same Victorian-style row house, ubiquitous throughout Shaw and Bloomingdale, that was sold for $8,000 in the 1950s is now on the market for $1.3 million (and the sale prices rise daily). According to a calculation by RENTCafé, a real estate analysis site, the zip code 20001 was the second fastest gentrifying area in the country between 2000 and 2016, judged by the increase in home values, household income level and proportion of residents with higher education.[1]

Countless articles have been written about the area, and I noticed something: the most common narrative simplified the dynamic to two groups—Black and White, poor and rich, original residents and gentrifiers. White people pushing out Black people.

For the past ten years, I've been living in this neighborhood and reporting on real estate and development for local publications. I realized that the situation was much more nuanced than that. The diversity of experience, perspective and feeling within both the Black community and the White gentrifier community was getting lost. Some of the first White people who moved in, paying $300,000 for their homes in the early 2000s, lived as racial minorities for years and had no expectation of fancy restaurants or cleaned-up public spaces. They could not be lumped into the same group as the newest gentrifiers, who paid $1.3 million for the same place and expected a sparkling, crime-free neighborhood with a luxurious atmosphere. Black renters who had been displaced when their landlords decided to sell at a profit were nowhere to be found in the neighborhood. Other Black residents who lived through the worst of the drug years were sitting on boards and in community meetings with White residents, planning arts festivals and demanding good grocery stores and neighborhood-serving amenities from developers. Others, who had worked hard to improve their neighborhoods during the crack epidemic, are now being looked at with suspicion by the new White neighbors. But at the same time, I saw interracial friendships blossom between people who had never lived in an integrated neighborhood before.

I knew that White gentrifiers were being blamed for displacing Black residents, and I did notice that numbers showed a shrinking Black population, and a growing White one. But at the same time, the stories I heard from the 1960s, 1970s and 1980s were of a drug-addled neighborhood full of vacant houses. The census numbers show a drop in overall population in the 1980s and 1990s and then a rise.

So, just how true was the typical gentrification narrative? What was the full story of living in this integrated neighborhood?

I felt the need to create a more comprehensive and truer portrait of this neighborhood, so I launched this oral history project. I sat in living rooms in the neighborhood row houses and listened as the owners told me about their personal histories. They shared the moments they chose to move here, their first impressions and their observations as the neighborhood went through wave after wave of change. They shared their unfiltered feelings: how safe they felt or didn't feel, how comfortable they were with their neighbors and what they expected from their neighborhood.

My goal was to be comprehensive in choosing interview subjects. I've arranged the book chronologically, starting with a narrator who was born in the area in the 1940s. From there, others enter the scene as they were either born here or moved in; every decade is populated, and my most recent narrators bought a home in 2020. Together, they describe a staggering change. The subjects of this book have seen this area go from a poor and peaceful neighborhood, to an open-air drug market and to a wealthy and amenity-filled space, and they have seen it go from full, to nearly vacant, to full again. Neighborhood schools were officially segregated, then school integration and White flight left them with de facto segregation, and now, they are integrating.

When Gretchen Wharton came to Shaw in 1946, the houses were full of families who looked like hers: lower income, Black, two parents with kids.

The sidewalks were full of children playing, and the mothers watched over them all from their windows and stoops.

When Leroy Thorpe moved in in the 1980s, the same streets were dense with drug markets. Hundreds of people crowded the streets, day and night, buying and using drugs and hiring prostitutes. Telephone booths were used for drug deals. Gunshots rang out from cars driving by, shooting at rivals.

When John Lucier, an Ohio-born government employee, found a deal on a house in Shaw in 2002, he found himself moving into one of the four occupied homes on a block of seventeen. Every morning, he walked alone to the newly opened metro station, waiting by himself on the empty platform. Census data shows the neighborhood had been emptied out.

When Preetha Iyengar became pregnant with her first child in 2016, she jumped into a seller's market to buy a row house in the area with her husband, losing one bidding war before winning another. As she walks down her block, she sees children playing on the spontaneous playground that emerged next to the pizza place on the corner. During the day, au pairs and nannies push children down the sidewalks, and housecleaners jump in and out of their cars to keep the houses of their wealthy clients looking immaculate.

At this moment, they are all still here, living alongside each other. Black, White and Asian residents talked to me about living in an integrated neighborhood for the first time in their lives. How do they build community in such diversity?

The narrators reflect deeply on their experiences of living alongside those of a different race. How do they experience respect? How do they experience belonging? "What happened to Black people in this neighborhood? I'm going to give it to you straight," said Leroy Thorpe, a powerful narrator you will first encounter in the 1980s section of this book. I hope you will read through to the end of the book, when he does give it to me straight and joins some of my earliest narrators with reflections about the most beautiful gains and the most painful losses of living in this neighborhood and when some of the most recent newcomers wonder about their responsibilities to their neighbors.

The heart of this book comes from the voices of the narrators. All the narrators in the project are using their real names and have graciously consented to allow me to publish their stories. I'm so grateful for their voices, which tell the truth of their experiences and their feelings.

With my gratitude, I offer my vulnerability: I include myself in the book, and I appear in the 2010s section, when I moved into the neighborhood.

I very much belong to the wave of gentrifiers who came in during that time, and I share many similarities with them; I know that many of my own biases will be exposed in that section. Since I asked my narrators to give me so much of themselves, I felt it was only fair to lay out all of my experiences, observations, hopes and fears as well. How do I fit into this community? You will find out.

The book is also punctuated by some very local context that I dug up and hope will help illuminate the narrators' stories. How did the forces of segregation shape the neighborhood? How did 1968 change Shaw? When did real estate developers jump into the neighborhood? When did the first stylish coffeeshop open up?

The oral history format will allow readers to feel that they are listening in on intimate conversations and hearing the unadulterated stories, thoughts and feelings of residents. I mainly conducted the interviews one on one, with the exception of married couples and two friends who wanted to be interviewed together. The voices are all woven together throughout the book. As different topics emerge—schools, public spaces, race relations— early narrators are threaded back in. My goal was to include as many voices as necessary to paint a complete picture, to have open conversations and to cover the full scope of life in this neighborhood from 1950 to 2021. I want the book to feel omniscient about the inner lives of the residents.

Hopefully, readers will feel liberated to come up with their own understanding of life in our gentrified neighborhood.

ACKNOWLEDGEMENTS

My deepest thanks go to my thirteen resident narrators. This book is composed of their stories and some of their most unfiltered thoughts and feelings about living here. I am humbled and so grateful that they shared them with me and now with the world. The book would very obviously not exist without them. Thank you so much to Gretchen Wharton, Greg Mason, Michelle Carthen, Leroy Thorpe, Scott Roberts, John Corea, John Lucier, Suki Lucier, Juan Laster, Christina Robbins, Ruxandra Pond, Preetha Iyengar, Nick Grube and Christina Papanicolaou.

This book also exists because of Kate Jenkins, the editor at Arcadia Publishing who first saw the value in this work.

It also exists because my sons, Hugo and Leo, brought me out of the house and into the neighborhood when they were young. The hours I spent in the area's public spaces, like its playgrounds, library and cafés, enhanced my understanding of the neighborhood and the community immeasurably. Being around the neighborhood throughout the day for so many years gave me access to hundreds of stories and helped me form connections that led directly or indirectly to my narrators.

Thank you to Jacquelyn Bengfort, a trusted friend and my first reader, who assured me that it all made sense and who gave me the gentle encouragement to keep gathering these stories and puzzling them together.

Thank you to Maggie Lemere, an oral historian who showed me a path that helped me learn more about this field, which I stumbled into sideways.

Her support for the project gave me the faith to keep pursuing it, and her push into the world of oral history led me to a much deeper understanding of what I was doing.

Thank you to Mark Wellborn and Will Smith, who hired me at *UrbanTurf* years ago and gave me a job that required me to get to know all the neighborhoods in Washington, D.C. All those hours spent in community meetings, scouring local blogs and talking to residents and developers for my *UrbanTurf* articles gave me the base of context on which this book rests.

Thanks also to Dion Haynes, my editor at the *Washington Post*, for giving me space to write several articles that helped me understand dynamic neighborhoods with diverse communities in them.

Thank you to the wonderful people who watched my children while I wrote this book: Miriam Ragen, Sera Stotelmyre and Maddy Sherbet.

Thank you to my two researchers: Beth Ferraro, who dug up historical photographs, and Sharita Thomas, who sifted through census and crime data. The book benefits greatly from their work.

Thank you to my mother, Shipra Paul, and my late father, Pradip Paul, who have given me many gifts that can never be repaid.

And thank you to my husband, Matt Malinowski, who gave me the space and time to work on this project during the plague year and whose constant support is my life's gift.

TIMELINE OF VOICES

1940   Gretchen Wharton

1950   Gregory Mason

1960   Michelle Carthen

1970

1980   Juan Laster
        Leroy Thorpe
        Scott Roberts

1990

2000   John Corea
        John and Suki Lucier

2010   Christina Robbins
        Shilpi Malinowski
        Ruxandra Pond
        Preetha Iyengar

2020   Nick Grube and Christina Papanicolaou

INTRODUCTION

What is a home? What does it mean to the people who live in it and to the people who buy and sell it? Is it a shelter: a source of comfort and a place to retreat from a wild and unpredictable world? Or is it an asset: a way to build wealth or a way to extract wealth? Is it both?

Through the process of putting this book together, I've come to believe that difference in definition—home or asset—lies at the heart of the tension surrounding gentrification.

As the decades go by, the prices of the same houses rise—this is gentrification at its most basic definition.

Many of my narrators live in very similar houses. In one case, the narrators have lived in the same house, their residency separated by twenty years. What happens when a house that had a previous value of $10,000 is now worth $30,000—then $300,000, then $1.3 million? How does our perception of that house change? How do the people who inhabit that house feel, and what do they expect from their home and neighborhood?

On one hand, I talked to a homeowner who lived in a completely paid-off house that had been in his family for fifty years. What he valued about his home was the safety of it and the constancy of its shelter. The home also connected him to the neighborhood and the people around him, and those relationships are meaningful and exist because of the home. When he was in the house, he remembered his parents and the memories of his childhood. If he had lived in that house until his death, to him, the house would never

Houses in LeDroit Park, mid-1900s. *Wm. Edmund Barrett, Kiplinger Washington Collection, D.C. History Center.*

have had any strong relationship to money. If he received an offer to leave the home, what would that money be replacing for him?

On the other hand, I share the story of a developer who saw the steep and seemingly constant rise in real estate prices in a gentrifying neighborhood and jumped into the market. They bought a house and added some features to it, though they were careful to contain their costs so they could sell it to a new homeowner at a profit. Because they planned to sell immediately after renovating it, they didn't have to consider the lasting quality of any of the features they added. To that developer, the home was solely an asset and a way to build their own wealth. In that transaction, where did that wealth come from?

For those who moved in toward the middle of the rise in prices, they may stand somewhere in the middle of the home-versus-asset spectrum. Did they know that prices were going to rise in this neighborhood and, in turn, see their home as an investment? How do they protect and defend that investment? For those who moved in very recently, their purchase price was so high that they don't consider it an investment; they have no reason to

Carter G. Woodson Memorial Park, Ninth Street and Rhode Island Avenue Northwest. *Shilpi Malinowski.*

Carter G. Woodson Memorial Park, Ninth Street and Rhode Island Avenue Northwest. *Shilpi Malinowski.*

believe they will sell it at a profit. The newest residents find themselves, much like the first residents, considering their house primarily as a home.

Realizing that the definition shifted helped me understand some of the feelings you will encounter in the narrators' stories.

RACE, VALUE AND GENTRIFICATION

As I learned more about segregation, integration and gentrification, untangling the relationship between race and housing value became a greater goal of mine.

In common practice until the 1940s was the addition a "racially restrictive covenant" to the deed of a house with language that made it illegal for the house to be sold to or occupied by Black people. Many houses in Washington, D.C., had those covenants attached to their deeds, and many neighborhoods became homogenously White; in neighborhoods where covenants didn't exist, Black people settled in.[2]

According to Sarah Shoenfeld, a Washington, D.C.–based historian who analyzes census data, maps, deeds and real estate records for her project "Mapping Segregation," covenants attached race to the value of property in a very explicit way. "It created value at no cost to developers," Shoenfeld told me, "simply by stating that these houses could never be sold to Black people. It created the idea that a house or neighborhood is worth more based on the race of the occupant who lives in the house."

As I dove deeper and deeper into this project, that value-based relationship nagged at me.

Over the last twenty years, the percentage of White residents in our neighborhood has risen. As the neighborhood became Whiter, housing prices rose.

Was there a sort of shadow relationship created by racially restrictive housing covenants in the early twentieth century that was playing out in gentrifying neighborhoods? Was each property worth more because it was then valuable to a White buyer?

The value difference can sometimes be seen explicitly.

The homes of White and Black homeowners are often appraised at different levels.[3] In one case, a Black couple in the Bay Area had their home appraised for $500,000 more once they removed family photographs and replaced them with those of a White friend.[4] In another case, an interracial couple in Florida found an appraisal difference of more than $100,000, depending on which one of them was present during the appraisal and which photographs were displayed.[5]

In 2020, the Appraisal Institute (AI) acknowledged the unconscious bias that may be influencing appraisers and started a conversation about it within the industry. "The process involves reinforcing zero tolerance for appraiser bias, exploring continuing education for focus on bias and racism awareness," said Jody Bishop, president-elect of AI, in a recent issue of their internal member publication.[6]

"The problem with housing being an asset and a very significant wealth-building asset is, for one, they appreciate at very different rates for White and Black people," said Shoenfeld. "So, this whole trope about homeownership being the primary means of accumulating wealth in this country—it has also been a primary means of stripping people of wealth. Because of the continued association of race with the value of property, it's almost like gentrification has necessitated the displacement of Black people. That's part of the value that has been created as the neighborhoods are now more White."

Part I

SEVENTY YEARS IN SHAW, LEDROIT PARK AND BLOOMINGDALE

1

1950s AND 1960s

Busy Sidewalks and Black Families

You could leave the door wide open, because everybody looked out for each other.
It was a family atmosphere.
—Greg Mason

A s we enter Shaw, LeDroit Park and Bloomingdale in the 1950s, Washington, D.C., is highly segregated.

According to Chris Myers Asch and George Derek Musgrove's definitive and detailed history *Chocolate City: A History of Race and Democracy in the Nation's Capital*, deed covenants were a popular method of maintaining segregation in Washington, D.C.

From the book:

> *Restrictive covenants proliferated in the wake of a 1917 supreme court decision that prohibited state and local governments from mandating segregation through zoning ordinances but did not address exclusionary agreements among private individuals.*
>
> *The North Capitol Citizen Association, which represented the Bloomingdale area, convinced nearly all neighborhood homeowners to sign covenants. Prospective Black home buyers were threatened with lawsuits, and if a covenant was broken, the association assumed the expenses of the ensuing legal challenge.*[7]

LeDroit Park mural *This is How We Live*, by artist Garin Baker. *Shilpi Malinowski.*

The use of covenants and the practice of redlining meant that Black families were restricted to certain neighborhoods in the District.

While the covenants ensured that Bloomingdale remained White, Shoenfeld told me that she has never found racially restrictive housing covenants in Shaw, leaving that area open for Black residents. "Blacks were already living in Shaw at the time that racial covenants came into use [the early 1900s]," Shoenfeld told me.

Nearby LeDroit Park, located just south of the Howard University campus, has a complicated history. The neighborhood was developed in the late 1800s as an exclusive neighborhood for White residents.[8] Once developed, the neighborhood was surrounded by a fence and guarded by hired watchmen.

But the proximity of the area to the renowned Black university became uncomfortable; in 1888, according to *Chocolate City*, "The ragged barrier was torn down and rebuilt several times in the next three years as a 'fence war' raged." The fence soon came down for good, and in 1893, the first Black resident bought a home in LeDroit Park. Within decades, the neighborhood had flipped: "By World War I, it was almost exclusively Black and would remain so for the rest of the twentieth century."[9]

LeDroit Park Gate, 2021. *Shilpi Malinowski.*

Bloomingdale Rowhouses, 2021. *Shilpi Malinowski.*

Now, the pressure turned to Bloomingdale. "Bloomingdale developed in an area that was surrounded on three sides by areas where Black people lived: Shaw, LeDroit and Howard Town," said Shoenfeld. "There is nice housing there, it's close to LeDroit and it's close to Howard. There was a lot of desire among Black families who had the ability to purchase property to live in Bloomingdale."

In a historic win for integration, Bloomingdale was the site of a case that ultimately brought down racially restrictive housing covenants. In 1944, a Black couple bought a home at 116 Bryant Street that was still tied to a racially restrictive deed covenant. When the neighbors attempted to sue, the case, *Hurd v. Hodge*, ended up going all the way up to the supreme court. In 1948, according to *Chocolate City*:

> *The court decided unanimously in May 1948 to overturn the lower courts' rulings in* Hurd v. Hodge, *finding that judicial enforcement of race-based restrictive covenants violated the Civil Rights Act of 1866 by limiting Black Washingtonians' equal right to own and use property. The covenants no longer were legally enforceable, and the Hurds could keep their home.*[10]

After the case made covenants illegal, Bloomingdale very quickly became a Black neighborhood. In 1950, according census data, the area that lines up with the zip code 20001 (which contains Shaw, LeDroit Park and Bloomingdale) was 82 percent Black and 18 percent White. By 1960, the same area was 92 percent Black.[11]

This is the scene where our story begins. All of the narrators included in this book live or have lived in Shaw, LeDroit Park or Bloomingdale.

We'll begin in Shaw.

Gretchen Wharton has seen the life of her neighborhood shift again and again. Elegantly dressed in her delicately decorated and immaculate row house, Wharton invited me into her living room in 2019 to share her story. Her neighbors, a couple with young children, introduced me to her when they heard I was putting together this chronicle. Wharton's story spans the length of the book.

Wharton was born in 1946. Now that she is retired, she serves as the chair of the board of Shaw Main Streets, a nonprofit organization dedicated to revitalizing the business corridors in Shaw, and she sits on the boards of other arts organizations across the city.

Gretchen Wharton, 2021. *Shilpi Malinowski.*

GRETCHEN WHARTON. *I grew up directly across the street. My parents moved there when I was six months old.*

This house was owned by a single woman, and many years ago, in the early 1960s, she wanted to sell it after her husband had passed. She came across the street to my mom, and I said: "I want to buy it." And I did.

I never left the neighborhood and stayed with my mother to help with her health issues. Finally, I decided, we are going to move across the street, and it took me six months to convince her. "Mother, you have the same phone number, the same zip code!" We moved together, and I took care of her until she passed.

When I grew up here, everybody was very close. It was never a high socioeconomic group, but the people who were here were close. If I was out in the front yard playing and my mother had to go inside, my next-door neighbor was always watching—everybody was watching out for everybody.

People knew each other. I played with the kids in the next block and around the corner. There were some areas my parents didn't allow me to go to and certainly not those outside of the immediate few blocks.

When I moved into the neighborhood in 2011, a tall man with a giant smile stopped by to introduce himself while I was watering my grass. I soon learned that Greg Mason was a constant presence on the block, doing handywork for one home, trimming the rose bushes at another and walking up and down the sidewalk all throughout the day.

Mason was born in Shaw in 1956 and has a long, complex history with the neighborhood. I learned his history slowly over years of knowing him. He sat with me for this interview in late 2020.

GREG MASON. *I was here for fifty years, and my parents—they were here forever. Oh, there were so many kids, so many kids. This block, and that block, we were very close knit.*

We looked out for each other back then. You could leave the door wide open because everybody looked out for each other. It was a family atmosphere. Everybody looked out for everybody. Didn't nobody have to worry about anybody coming in your house or doing anything to anybody, because this block and that block was always a safe zone.

We wouldn't let no outside guys come in the neighborhood and talk to the females. They were like our little sisters or little cousins. If you wanted to talk to some guy, you had to meet him at Kennedy Playground, but they couldn't come here in the neighborhood.

Greg Mason, 2021. *Shilpi Malinowski.*

Every Halloween, there was a line around that corner up the street. My mother baked cookies. She would start the day before Halloween and just bake cookies. Everybody came to get them cookies. And then, as they got older, the children from way back got older, so their kids came. Their parents still came and got cookies, too.

My mother was everybody's mother around here.

Do you see where a blue awning is hanging over right there on Fourth Street, near Florida Avenue Northwest? That used to be Mr. Palmers; we used to go there and get ice cream cones, you know, we have five-cent cones, ten-cent cones. This was Sealtest—that was top of the line back in the day.

Over there, that used to be a laundry. Not a laundromat, but just a laundry where you would take your bedsheets and linen. They would clean them, press them, fold them and everything and wrap them up in that brown paper—that heavy brown paper—and put a string around them like that.

On the corner where the daycare center is, that used to be a bakery. Saturday morning, you get up, the breeze is coming this way, and you smell that. We had a Wonder Bread Bakery up on Georgia Avenue, right? That scent would come down. Oh man—you talk about something smells good.

Wonder Bread Factory, 1950s. *Emil A. Press slide collection, D.C. History Center.*

Wonder Bread Factory, 2021. *Shilpi Malinowski.*

Kennedy Recreation Center, 1950s. *Emil A. Press slide collection, D.C. History Center.*

We used to go swimming up at Banneker Swimming Pool [at the public recreation center]. And after we left the swimming pool, we'll go by the Wonder Bread Factory, and they said, "Look at all the day-old stuff; take as much as you want." They give us big old trash bags. We come down here, we gave all the kids Hostess cupcakes and the pies and everything because they can't sell it. They didn't want to throw it away, so they gave it to us.

That was a good time.

GRETCHEN WHARTON. *I went to public school all in this area—Scott Montgomery and Bundy Elementary School. People said, "Oh, my god, Bundy College, school of no knowledge." Not when I was there! We had a strict curriculum and major theater performances that people came to from around the city.*

I went to Shaw Junior High. People say, "You went to Shaw?" And I stayed up until 2 o'clock in the morning in seventh, eighth and ninth grade doing my homework, and we had teachers who were so driven that we had no choice but to study hard. I had to submit both math and science fair projects every year.

Asbury Dwellings, formerly Shaw Junior High, 2021. *Shilpi Malinowski.*

GREG MASON. *I went to Bundy Elementary School; then I left there and went to Shaw Junior High School. And then I graduated from there, and I went to Cardozo High School. I didn't want to go to Dunbar High School, although Dunbar was right down the street from here. But I wanted to meet a new group of people. You know, because I might not have did so well in school being around my friends. So, I went to Cardozo, and I played football up there for three years.*

Then I went to the Lincoln Technical Institute. I graduated, and I got a job at the Washington Gas Line Company, and then I was there for the next sixteen years.

GRETCHEN WHARTON. *From Shaw, I went to McKinley Tech. McKinley Technical High School integrated—I think—in 1954. When I got there in 1960, there weren't that many Whites. It changed that quickly. It was totally wild.*

McKinley was one of the schools that you could go to and take classes in advanced biology, pre-engineering, lab techniques. [Before the 1954 Brown vs. the Board of Education supreme court case ruled that segregated schools were unconstitutional, McKinley Tech was an all-White school.]

GREG MASON. *My parents were renting at some point. And then, one day, I heard Mom say to my father, "Look, the landlord came by and said, 'If you can't buy the house, you're gonna have to move.'" So, my father said, "Don't worry about that. Get your butt up in the morning to go to the bank and get the money."*

And that's what she did. That's what she did. She did it. That was in the 1960s. She went down and got the money. Got $24,000 cash out of the bank, and bought the house—no problem [$24,000 in 1962 would be equivalent to $215,356 in 2021 dollars, according to the U.S. Bureau of Labor Statistics CPI Inflation Calculator].[12]

My father said the reason they did that is so I would always have a place to live.

We had the streetcar line on R Street and the bus line. The streetcar went all the way to Massachusetts Avenue, toward the observatory. And that's how my mother got to work, you know, on the streetcar line or the bus line. It depends on which job she was going to.

My mother did domestic work here in the city and in Montgomery County, up Connecticut Avenue, at the Kennedy Warren. And they looked out for my mother, took care of my mother, everything. They always brought her home on Thanksgiving. The lady that was the cook was Miss Jackson; I called her Blackjack. My mother didn't have to cook Thanksgiving and Christmas dinner because there was so much food that she was bringing home.

GRETCHEN WHARTON. *In the late 1950s, Shaw had started to change because heroin traffic moved in first—probably in the late 1950s. In the early 1960s, nobody wanted houses around here—nobody. It was horrible.*

This was before crack; it was the heroin market. The guy who ran the trade for a large part of the city lived a block away. Everybody knew who he was; he knew everybody—he took care of the older people in the neighborhood. For Thanksgiving and Christmas, he made sure everybody had turkey dinners. He basically kept his trade away from the immediate neighbors.

It got very rough. There were shootings, in the 1960s especially, because of the drug traffic. Many people left. Many moved to Maryland. Many moved to Michigan Park [in northeast Washington, D.C.] *and Shepherd Park* [in northwest Washington, D.C.], *where it was nice and quiet, and they couldn't believe I was still here in Shaw.*

There were times that we didn't have a grocery store, only small corner convenience stores. My mother went to Eighteenth Street and Columbia Road Northwest for a full-service grocery store. When Giant finally came to our neighborhood, replacing the historic O Street Market, it was terrible. I personally called the health department and Giant Corporate when I went in there one day, reached up to get something off a shelf and all sorts of rodent droppings fell on me. Senior management met me the next day to address the issue.

There were many vacant and boarded homes in the 1960s and 1970s. It was not a comfortable feeling. My mom and my neighbor were the neighborhood watch. It was crazy for a while. Nobody slept at night. You didn't walk around the neighborhood. No, no, no, no—we didn't do that.

My friends still said, "How can you stay in the neighborhood now that it has changed?" And my mother said, "No one is running me out of my neighborhood."

Census data bears out Wharton's observations; between 1950 and 1960, the population of the same section of zip code 20001 dropped from 73,888 to 55,765.[13]

Wiltberger Street Northwest, 2021. *Shilpi Malinowski.*

O Street Market, 1950s. *Emil A. Press slide collection, D.C. History Center.*

Giant at O Street Market, 2021. *Shilpi Malinowski.*

GREG MASON. [The drug activity] *doesn't bother me. I didn't care because I knew all of them. You know—I mean—they were surviving. My brother, he died of a drug overdose. The way that we were raised back in that era was, number one, we were taught about death. That was instilled in our mind; that's gonna happen.*

GRETCHEN WHARTON. *When I grew up here, my dad used to give some of the young men quarters if they would pick up trash and put it in bags, just to give them something to do. Every Friday, there would be a line of people coming to the door. And unfortunately, some of them ended up being drug dealers. I knew them from when they were growing up.*

GREG MASON. *Oh, the neighborhood, it got a little rowdy. I remember, one day, me, my mother and my father were sitting here on the porch, and all of a sudden, we see this joker run out the alley right there. And somebody behind him pulled out one gun and shot him once and, just before he turned the corner right here, shot him again. The guy kept on running—he kept on running. I think he fell somewhere up there around block or something like that.*

But the neighborhood really wasn't never bad-bad, because all of us were so close around here. And then, we wouldn't let no outsiders come.

When my mother passed [in 2000], during that time, the drug activity was kind of heavy around here. But it wasn't bad. They wouldn't bother nobody; they were trying to get what they were trying to get.

Some of the addicts came by: "Hey, Mr. Mason, I'm sorry to hear about your mom. I just come by to bring you a little something-something." So, they might drop off a pint of this, a pint of this, a six-pack of this. Everybody surrounded me. Everybody came together, you know. "We got to look out for Mason."

When my mother passed, I had to go through this house and get all of this stuff out of the house. One of her hobbies was she collected TIME Magazines. *And she used to have bundles. She had so many; she had ten in a stack that she tied it up. And she had them up underneath her bed. I had to go through every magazine, every paper and shake it. One day, I'm shaking my magazines. I think I started at about 8 o'clock that morning. By 12 o'clock, I had found $4,000. Although my mother believed in banks, but that was just house money—that was emergency money. That was just the money I found falling out of magazines. In total, I think I found maybe about $20,000.*

When we were kids, an old lady died; she had this old car in her garage. She had one of those old cars that you crank in the front. And she had this old piano in the hallway. Oh man, that thing was old. Old people sometimes didn't believe in banks. We went in, and we found so much money in the piano—that was crazy. In the piano, that's where she stored it. That's where she hid her money. That was her bank right there.

GRETCHEN WHARTON. *When the riots came* [in 1968], *it was right here on Seventh Street; there was smoke all over this block—everywhere. People running up and down and breaking windows in the stores—it was really bad. People were breaking in stores and stealing, and it was so sad because we are reacting to this and destroying our own Black neighborhood—what are you doing? It looked like a bomb had gone off.*

It was so bad, and I kept thinking, "This is not going to be a quick recovery."

2

1970s AND 1980s

The Postriot Era

The neighborhood was very quiet.
—Michelle Carthen

On April 4, 1968, at 7:05 p.m., Dr. Martin Luther King Jr. was shot; within an hour, his death was announced to a stunned world. A few hours later, riots broke out around Washington, D.C.[14]

In his book *Most of 14th Street Is Gone*, J. Samuel Walker lays out a detailed, block-by-block breakdown of how the 1968 riots played out in Washington, D.C. Just blocks from Gretchen Wharton's home, "on the Seventh Street Corridor, stretching from Florida Avenue as far south as Pennsylvania Avenue, roving bands of rioters shattered windows at more than eighty stores, including two department stores, Hecht's and Kann's."[15]

The 1968 riots had a profound impact on the population and demographics of the neighborhood. According to census data, the area roughly mapping out 20001 had a population of 55,764 in 1960; by 1970, the same area had a population of 39,893. The number of White people dropped from 3,810 to 881.[16] By 1980, the total population had dropped even further to 33,800. Vacant houses filled the blocks. In this chapter, the narrators tell us a story about their lives during this quiet stage—going to school, supporting each other—and how they coexisted with increasing drug activity.

Michelle Carthen, 2021. *Shilpi Malinowski.*

MICHELLE CARTHEN. *In the 1970s, that put me in elementary school. The neighborhood was very quiet. I like to call it the* Leave It to Beaver *era. Everybody worked; there were families playing on the street. It was a true village. Everybody took care of everybody's kids. We all had to be in the house by the time the streetlights came on. It was that kind of community.*

We played things that you don't even see anymore. We played hopscotch— we got chalk and wrote on the sidewalk and played hopscotch. We did a lot of double Dutch. We used to play in the alley; we played kickball. We rode our bicycles from U Street to V Street—that was as far as we could go.

In the 1970s, there was a very, very huge sense of community.

At First and Thomas Streets—there's a condo there now—that actually used to be a carry-out shop. They had the best chicken wings with mumbo sauce and French fries. Where the cleaners is, that used to be a hardware store. My mother would send us there to buy screws. The laundromat was where Red Hen is. That's where we used to do laundry because we didn't have a washing machine.

At First and T Streets, that used to be a place called Ts, and you could go there and get the best egg and cheese with French fries. It was Black-owned, the hardware store was Black-owned. All of them were Black-owned.

The Crispus Attucks Park Building—there used to be a recreation center right there. Grants were given to a neighborhood organization that allowed the neighborhoods to have community after-school activities for kids.

In the 1970s, neighbors banded together to take over an abandoned telephone switching station in the alley bounded by North Capitol Street Northwest, U Street Northwest, V Street Northwest and First Street Northwest. They formed a nonprofit organization and opened up the Crispus Attucks Park of the Arts Community Center to serve the children of the neighborhood.[17]

MICHELLE CARTHEN. *I was told that that building was given to this community for one dollar. It was designed for the purpose of making sure that kids had after-school activities. We used to call it the Cave Yard; you go over there and do your homework or whatever indoor activities that were available. There was tutoring available. The focus was on the kids and making sure that we had something to do and that we stayed out of trouble.*

My mom, she made sure that we stayed together. You go to school together; you walk together. But if somebody was bothering the other one, we would fight together. You walk away, try to keep peace as much as you can. But if you have to defend yourself, you fight together. So, that's how we've been raised—to be very close and very cohesive.

I went to Gage Eckington Elementary School, then I went to Shaw Middle School, then I went to Dunbar High School—it was one of the crème de la crème schools at the time. It's different now—very different.

And after I graduated from Dunbar, I went to Howard University. And then I learned that there were so many other things that Black people were doing—that Black people are doing well outside of my neighborhood. You go to Howard, and they teach you that you can do all these great things and that you can be this amazing person.

Above: Crispus Attucks, 1978. *Ward Bucher, AIA.*

Left: Dunbar High School, 1950s. *Emil A. Press slide collection, D.C. History Center.*

In 1981, Juan Laster bought her first home in nearby Bloomingdale. Laster grew up in West Virginia and came to Washington, D.C., to attend college at the University of the District of Columbia (UDC).

JUAN LASTER. *I bought this house when I was in college. I have a mentor who said to me, "You're not going to be twenty-one and cute forever. You need to plan for your future."*

I grew up on a farm in West Virginia in the mountains. My dad didn't want me to come to the big city, where the bad people are. My mom convinced him to let me come. I was a first-time graduate in my family.

My mom's best friend, she was up here. We became friends and she said, "Why don't you come and see what you can do?" I said, "I don't know." I was scared. My brother-in-law brought me downtown, and I was afraid to cross the street. I'd never seen so many people in all my life. I was like, "How do you cross the street?" And he said, "Red light, green light."

I was just overwhelmed by all the people that I saw—all kinds of different types of people. At UDC, I started with my AA and my bachelor's, then I got to my master's degree and graduated magna cum laude.

This neighborhood chose me; I didn't choose it. I think I looked in the Washington Post; *[my realtor] showed me a couple of houses, and we came here. I liked the house because it was quaint and just big enough for me.*

I didn't pay attention to the neighborhood; I was more, "I got a house!" I moved in on New Year's Eve; ice was everywhere, and they had taken the refrigerator—they left with it. I was really disappointed. I put all my food out on the back porch. The neighborhood was Ward 5—that's what it was. It was just Ward 5. I paid about $57,000 for the house.

My immediate neighbor used her house as a rooming house for Howard University students. Twenty dollars per room, per week. That's all she charged.

I had no clue this neighborhood was going to flourish the way that it has.

They used to sell drugs down at the corner store on Flagler Place Northwest. Across the street, the people who used to live there—I think it was a small family—he bought a dog and put the dog in the yard, so the dog would rush up to the fence and bark. And then [another neighbor] Sonya, was like, "No, not on my watch." She had a Doberman. So, the drug dealers kind of got the word out that the neighborhood is changing a little bit here.

Juan Laster, 2021. *Shilpi Malinowski.*

When I moved in, there was a vacant lot next to my house, and people hung out there to do their thing. So, that scared me a little bit, and I thought, "What have I done?" But there was no way I was going to move. No. Because everybody in my hometown knew that I purchased a home—my father made sure of that. They announced it in church. So, how could I move?

Leroy Thorpe served as an Area Neighborhood Commission (ANC) commissioner in Shaw for twenty years, from 1986 until 2006. As a commissioner, he was elected to represent an area with about two thousand residents, and he sat on a commission that met once a month to discuss neighborhood issues and send recommendations to the city. His name adorns iron tree boxes around the sidewalks of Shaw, and he can be spotted on his motorcycle every afternoon as he picks up his daughter from school.

Leroy Thorpe. *One of the pledges I made as an ANC commissioner was: "We want to clean up the drugs." And I did.*
You are talking about the 1980s—you would see two hundred people walking down here from Fifth and R Streets, up to P street, two hundred

Leroy Thorpe, 2021. *Shilpi Malinowski.*

people. Crackheads, drug dealers, just out on the street. Drive-by shootings, that kind of thing. All kinds of prostitution in terms of female prostitution, and male prostitutes dressed like women. So, I closed all these crack houses down, man. I really started making progress. In 2002, I shut the last one down; I shut down fifty-six of them.

My process was like this: you go there, you harass them, you get the DCRA going in and citing them for violations. Most of the houses were in bad shape. They were not really livable.

Those folks who were going there using as guests of the hosts would leave, and eventually, the owner would have to give it up because they can't afford all the repairs and fines. That was the process.

Also, we removed all the telephone booths that were around there; people would use them for transactions. Drug dealers would say, "Go to the telephone booth, put the money in the slot. And I'll get the money and then put your drugs in there."

Then, sometimes, they would have Coke cans, put the crack cocaine in there.

I took pictures of the drug dealers I ran into, and the police would come and say, "Let me see your pictures." I had all the equipment—the police had to go through red tape, but I had all the equipment: cameras, binoculars. So, they would say, "Let's go through Thorpe's pictures."

I have patrol groups. The police would come and get me, and we would raid apartment buildings.

People were scared of me. They respected me, because one thing about me is if I say I'm going to do something, I do it. If you are out on the street, and you say you are going to do something and you don't do it, you lose credibility. And I never took a bribe. The [dealers] said: "Man, what do you want, what do you want?" And I said: "I'm not taking a penny from you, then you got me." So, my integrity was intact.

Wherever I went, they were like, "It's Thorpe—let's go."

Thorpe's patrol groups, officially called COPE (Citizen Organized Patrol Efforts) and known informally as the "Red Hats," attracted attention during the 1990s. In 2004, the *Washington Times* described their "in-your-face" tactics, confronting dealers in alleys, holding loud protests in front of crack houses and rallying city officials and police to conduct raids and evict users and dealers from dilapidated houses.[18]

And in a 2005 *Washington Times* article, "Shaw Neighbors Honor Samaritan," neighbors joined Police Chief Charles Ramsey in applauding Thorpe's commitment to neighborhood safety.

From the article:

> *"At one time, the neighborhood was infested with drugs and crime," Lillian Gordan, a Shaw resident for 55 years, recalled yesterday at the annual Shaw Awards Block Party. "Everything was terrible. There was a time when hundreds of people were walking through the community selling and buying drugs."*
>
> *"It was awful, and a lot of people moved out because of it....Leroy cleaned up the drugs in our community, and he almost did it single-handedly. The drug boys were scared of him. They said: 'He didn't mind dying.'"*[19]

3

1990s

A Crack Epidemic Blankets the Neighborhood

You'd see these station wagons drive around with one or two people sitting in the front, the back seat pushed down and the entire rest of the back of the station wagon was filled with machine guns and rifles, filled up to the windows.
—*Scott Roberts*

Crack cocaine loomed large in Washington, D.C., in the 1990s—on the streets, in the news and in the halls of power. Kicking off the decade in January 1990 was the much-publicized arrest of then–Washington, D.C. mayor Marion Barry for possessing cocaine.[20] Barry had been mayor for more than a decade at that point, having been elected in 1978 after gaining recognition as a civil rights leader and then as a councilmember. Despite his arrest and history with crack cocaine, he was re-elected to the city council in 1993 and served again as mayor from 1995 to 1999.

Why were D.C. residents so fond of the fallible Barry? According to Chris Myers Asch and George Derek Musgrove's history *Chocolate City: A History of Race and Democracy in the Nation's Capital*, Barry was initially elected with the support of disparate groups. "Many White voters viewed him as a break from the past, a man tough enough to deal with both the Black poor and White business interests," they noted, and the *Washington Post* threw their support behind him.[21]

GRETCHEN WHARTON. *Marion Barry created the Black middle class in this city. All the Black people who live in Colonial Village and upper Sixteenth Street, he gave them jobs, he enabled them to get contracts with the city. That didn't happen before. There was a big difference. Some of the changes spun off of Barry—people don't want to give him credit, but they did.*

As mayor, Barry created many initiatives that, as Wharton recalled, are credited with building the Black middle class back up in Washington, D.C. "He wanted local government to work for people—particularly low-income Black residents—who had been locked out of decision making since Reconstruction," said Asch and Musgrove.

From their book:

> *The city's population was roughly 70 percent Black, but minority-owned businesses held only 7 percent of the city contracts in 1978. Minority Business Opportunity Commission director Courtland Cox intended to more than triple that number immediately, warning that city agency directors who failed to give 25 percent of their contracts to minorities "should seriously evaluate their positions in city government." Barry leaned hard on White contractors, telling them that they must hire Black workers if they wanted city business.*[22]

During this decade, the neighborhood, like the mayor, was on a journey of hard-fought growth amid the chaos and lure of crack cocaine and the drug market.

The demographics of the area covered in this book didn't change much between 1980 and 1990; according to census data, the total population was at a nadir, but it was stable, going from 33,800 in 1980 to 33,404 in 1990, and there was a slight increase in the population of White residents, from 1,256 to 1,937.

However, some other changes were brewing; in 1991, the Shaw-Howard University Metro Station opened on Seventh Street Northwest, with entrances at S Street Northwest and R Street Northwest. The station was one factor that made the area more appealing to developers, and once the station was in place, residential apartments, large and small, began to spring up near the entrances.[23]

Scott Roberts moved to LeDroit Park in 1989, moving east from Foxhall Village on the far western side of the city. Roberts is the unofficial historian of Bloomingdale and the surrounding area; he maintains the neighborhood blog and listserv, where he notes new developments, crimes, houses for sale

Metro construction on the 1200 Block of U Street Northwest. *Zinnia*, DC Changes, *photograph collection, D.C. History Center.*

and shops opening up. His fast-walking, slender frame topped with wild white hair has been a ubiquitous sight on the streets during the decade that I've lived here. I met Roberts before I moved into the neighborhood; as a local blogger, I often scoured neighborhood blogs to catch hyperlocal news before it spread more widely, and I was a fan of his *Bloomingdale Neighborhood Blog.*[24] He sat down with me at a local café in 2019 for this interview.

At the time that Roberts moved to the area, drug dealing was a common sight around the streets.

> SCOTT ROBERTS. *The day I moved in from my rental house in Foxhall Village to my rental house on Third Street Northwest in LeDroit Park, I didn't have a car. I was unloading a van, and these guys with knives came up to me. They didn't actually stand there and threaten me; they just stood there as I was moving in. They didn't want me moving into the house.*

Scott Roberts, 2021. *Shilpi Malinowski.*

They stood there on the sidewalk holding the knives out. They didn't say anything threatening, but they stood there with knives, and they were pointing them at me. I had three or four trips. Every time I pulled up my van to unload, they would be sitting on the sidewalk; they would recognize the van, and they would stand there again. They didn't want me to move there.

The 300 block of T Street Northwest at that time was a complete open-air drug market. Oh, it was terrifying.

Remember the old A&W Root Beer stands? You would drive your car up to a little area and a teenage girl in roller skates would come out and take your order, and when your order was ready, she would roller-skate out with the root beer on a plate, go to your window and you sat and ate in your car? That's what it was like. You just drive up, and people just exchange drugs for money out in the open on the street.

I had no clue.

So, the reason the guys didn't want me to move there was because it was a drug market, and they didn't want anyone watching.

My house got broken into; I had a bunch of stuff in the basement. You could tell they spent hours—it wasn't a dash and run. They were sitting there for hours going through every single box and picked the stuff they wanted.

It was an adventure. I liked Foxhall Village, but it was safe, and nothing happens there. And I wanted to buy a house; I loved the architecture.

You walk around and realize there are virtually no White people here. The first week or two, you walk down the streets and get to know your neighbors. At Quincy Place Northwest, at the bottom of the neighborhood, the most southern street, I was walking down the street, and this old Black gentleman came up to me and said: "Oh, hello, you are the new White man who moved onto W Street."

Everybody was just talking. "Another White person is moving to the neighborhood." There was nothing bad at all about it. He introduced himself; he said, "Welcome to the neighborhood." And I thought, "Wow, this is really different."

When I moved onto my block, there were a few other White people on my block. The real estate agent who wanted me to buy my house lived on the corner. I was a total victim. He was a realtor, he was White, he wanted me to move around the block to have company because I was White. A year later, he left—he got what he wanted. He wanted to increase the percentage of the White people. I don't know; it breaks 10 percent and magic happens, money falls from heaven, I don't know.

So, I ended up buying a house on W Street Northwest. And I came home from settlement, and the guys who were renting there—there was crap everywhere: pizza boxes on the floors, spaghetti on the walls, condoms everywhere, pot stuff everywhere. I opened the back door from the kitchen, and there were people having sex. Did they stop? No. You are going to stand there until you are done. OK, let's get a phone, call a contractor, let's get a fence installed. I found spent bullets in the house, used needles.

The first night I was there, I hear a knock on the door at 2 o'clock in the morning. What's going on? There is no AC, I had the windows open. The guys who rented the house owed the drug dealer some money. They were all Howard University students.

I stick my head out, and the guy said, "Who the hell are you?"

I say, "Under new management. I just bought the house today."

"Where are the guys?"

"They're not here anymore."

Again, this was before the internet; there were no email addresses, they didn't give me phone numbers—they disappeared, they left.

I said, "I don't know where they are."

And he said, "I'm getting my money one way or the other. I'm coming back tomorrow night, and I'm getting my money one way or the other."

And I just said, "I'm sorry. I just bought the house; I went to settlement today. I don't know where they are."

I thought, "OK, he's going to come back, and he's going to kill me, and that's it." Thankfully, he didn't show up.

So, that's what it was like in the early 1990s.

I had a block matron. She hung out on the stoop for three or four or five hours a day. She knew everybody: she knew who was going to prison, who was getting out of prison, who was having whose baby, who was selling drugs, who was buying drugs, who was using drugs. She knew everybody. She knew who was a thief—she knew everything and everybody.

She gave me an education.

GRETCHEN WHARTON. *My mom's bedroom was on the ground floor, and I remember, one night, thinking: "She's never going to get any sleep." They are right in front of the house, fifteen of them, making noises, breaking bottles, not to mention the drugs. I wasn't going to call the police, because you just don't do that…everybody would know who called. So, I walked over to Wiltburger Street to have a discussion with the head drug dealer. And I told him who I was, and he said: "Are you Mrs. Wharton's daughter?" And*

I said: "My mother is sick, and she can't sleep at night." And he moved everybody. After that night, there wasn't another drug dealer on our block of S Street. He relocated that group. The police couldn't have done that.

And everyone asked me, "You went up there?" And I said: "What else was I supposed to do?"

Crime was not good. There needed to be a singular focus on crime. But that wasn't going to happen until the neighborhood started changing. Case in point, Sursum Corda [a public housing project]. *I remember when it was being built, and I thought it was going to be so wonderful, these little peaceful courtyards—all that did was hide the drug dealers. I'm just glad to see it go.* [The Sursum Corda development has since been demolished to make way for a mixed-income development funded by the D.C. Housing Finance Agency.][25]

SCOTT ROBERTS. *Half the houses were unoccupied—they were empty. Some squatters—I remember on Flagler Place Northwest, you had the drugged squatters, high on crack or whatever. They are high on drugs; they would find a place and move in. Then it's wintertime, and they need heat, so they find some furniture and start a fire in the house. The exterior is brick, but there's wood everywhere! They could burn the entire block down. There was no internet or anything, so I had to go to DCRA and say: "They are here right now—you have to come now—they are going to burn down the house; you have to come before sunset today."*

Part of what was going on was stolen cars. If you steal a car, you want to spray paint it a different color, so it looks like a different car. So, the way they detailed it is to do it on the street in front of everybody. It's 2 o'clock in the morning, they have a generator for lights, you hear this grrrrrrrrrr for hours. They don't even do it in a garage with some kind of cover; they just did it in the street.

Then the MPD was working with the national guard. They would have these gigantic flatbed trucks and these gigantic lights that you use to illuminate skyscrapers in Manhattan. They would shine those up into the sky on a really heavy-duty drug day. I remember coming home from work one days, and there were three on the block.

"Oh, my god, I'm in Beirut! The only thing missing was bombs coming from the sky. This is a military state. Is my block really that bad of a drug block?" In fact, it was.

You'd see these station wagons drive around with one or two people sitting in the front, the back seat pushed down and the entire rest of the

1200 Block of Seventh Street Northwest, 1950s. *Emil A. Press slide collection, D.C. History Center.*

back of the station wagon was filled with machine guns and rifles, filled up to the windows. Seventy-five to one hundred of them. You'd think that they would take a blanket and cover them up!

In 1994, there was a program where [MPD] *partnered with the National Park Service. They have a police unit. All they did was drive around looking for stuff to arrest people. The National Park Service police were not on radio call like MPD.*

So, the National Park Service would stop these vehicles....They would take a right turn without a signal, and they would stop them. And they'd see this stack of seventy-five weapons, and it's like "OK, I guess we're going to arrest you for that!"

And then they could get something special for a forty-eight-hour period where you could just stop vehicles just to do it. When they did that, they would post these gigantic fluorescent orange signs and announce it. The realtors hated it. They were like, "Can we tear these down?"

That whole stretch of Seventh and Ninth Streets was just one big drug zone. This is horrible, but a group of friends said: "Let's go over to Ninth street in the daytime on a Saturday and just walk around." I thought: "Oh, my god, let's park on Eighteenth Street because we are afraid we will get killed." We walked there, and there were drugs and prostitutes everywhere. It was really dangerous. That's what it was; there were prostitutes everywhere. It was a parking garage in the middle of the block where Whole Foods is now located, and people would go there and have sex all the time. It was Sexville.

One more early 1990s thing—there was drug dealing shift work. At the corner of First and W Streets, you would see guys on each corner standing there for several hours, selling stuff to people who would drive up. They would be there for four to six hours; then a station wagon would pull up, three or four guys would get out, and the guys who had been standing there would get in. So, there was factory shift work going on all throughout the day.

They would wear crazy stuff—stripes and plaids and mismatched shoes and mismatched gloves—like, "We need to take you to a fashion consultant!" Throughout the day, they would switch the hat and switch the coats and change the socks and whatever—to make it so that if you called the police and said, "The guy with the purple scarf and green coat." No, he's switched things around.

The most notorious block in the neighborhood was the unit block of T Street Northwest. I worked out in Herndon. I told people where I lived— these are people who come to the city once a year when their relatives visit, to go to the Washington Monument—and even the suburbanites know this! They are not drug people; they knew about T Street!

It was notorious.

MICHELLE CARTHEN. *My oldest was born right in the midst of the crack epidemic.*

I had my five pillars: I wanted them to get out of the city alive, drug-free, baby-free, disease-free and record-free.

The oldest one, he went off to college on scholarship, and so did the youngest one. It was hard because, in order to do that, you have to give up yourself—you have to give up your life.

Some of my best friends and family members were allegedly part of the whole drug thing. So, you have this conflict about: "Wow, y'all are possibly tearing down the neighborhood." And I'm raising my little Black boys. But we are all family. [My sons] saw this glam life versus "we've got to work hard and figure it out."

That's hard—to teach a young boy to just stay focused, get their education. They see it now, of course, because some of those people [associated with the drug market] *are no longer here—they are dead. Or they're still just out there doing the same thing. And then, you know, we know them; we're still family, so they also look after us, and they protect us, and they make sure that we are okay.*

They respect my sons because they didn't do it their way.

I think with them not going to the neighborhood school, that probably helped—it probably did help. So, you know, the exposure was a little bit different.

They went to Stevens Elementary School downtown and then D.C. Prep [a charter school]. *D.C. Prep was a godsend.*

When my oldest graduated from D.C. Prep, they connected the students to really great resources, so he ended up going to a boarding school for two years. Then he came back and he went to School Without Walls [an application high school in D.C.].

My youngest went to McKinley Technology High School [another application school].

In 1998, Charles Ramsey took on the role of metropolitan police chief of D.C. Over the course of his eight-year tenure, the overall crime rate in the city went down by 40 percent, according to his biography on the Metropolitan Police Department's website.[26]

Ramsey had a few strategies: he increased the number of officers patrolling neighborhoods and created tangible partnerships between police and the community with a focus on community policing. The National Police Foundation defines community policing as a sort of preventative practice; police develop relationships with the community and identify problems, rather than solely responding to serious crime incidents.[27] Ramsey's initiative, "Policing for Prevention," existed within that philosophy.

Ramsey and his officers worked closely with neighbors, including Leroy Thorpe and his Red Hats in Shaw. In 2004, Thorpe presented a Red Hats Award to Chief Ramsey, as noted in a *Washington Times* article: "'He deserves national recognition,' Mr. Thorpe said, adding that while much of the D.C. government does little to work with volunteer crime-watch groups, Chief Ramsey 'is the only guy that utilizes [them].'"[28] According to data from the MPD, incidents of violent crime in the city dropped from 8,539 in 2000 to 6,323 in 2010.

Later in his career, Ramsey was chosen to cochair President Barack Obama's task force on twenty-first century policing.

SCOTT ROBERTS. *The open-air ridiculous drug dealing stuff changed.*

4

2000s

Houses Are Flipped, Trees Are Planted and the First Café Opens

Gentrification started coming in, because I looked at my numbers as I was running for office. And my numbers were going down in terms of the high percentage points. As the White folks were coming in, my numbers were going down.
—*Leroy Thorpe*

D uring this decade, the city, real estate developers and entrepreneurs laid the groundwork that dramatically changed Shaw, LeDroit Park and Bloomingdale.

The zip code 20001 started off the decade with a population of 33,216, similar to 1990. But within ten years, the zip code increased its population by almost 20 percent, ending with 39,296 in 2010. The population growth continues to this day.

Mayor Anthony Williams, who took office in 1999, pushed real estate development throughout the city, and real estate speculators zeroed in on the area. According to a 2017 interview in the *Washington Post*, Williams helped attract $27 billion in real estate investment to the city during his first four-year term.[29] In 2003, aside from stating a goal of attracting 100,000 residents to move to Washington, D.C., Williams was at the helm when the Washington Convention Center opened on the southern end of Shaw. According to a 2004 mayoral press release, the convention center brought in $426.5 million in its first year of operation.[30]

As Williams stated in a *Post* interview, "I thought the number-one thing to do was to create a climate where people were willing to reinvest in

D.C....Once you create a flow of investment, you start solving financial problems. But first, you have to improve the operation of the place, and then you can start creating a cycle of prosperity."[31]

According to the book *Chocolate City*:

> [Williams] *encouraged the Department of Housing to seize abandoned buildings and sell them to developers; auctioned off city-owned properties, including old schools and post offices; worked with Metro to spur development around transit centers; pushed the U.S. Small Business Administration to find ways to revitalize neighborhood commercial centers; and begged federal lawmakers to transfer huge parcels, such as St. Elizabeth's Hospital, Walter Reed Army Medical Center and the Navy Yard, to the city so that it could build entirely new communities.*[32]

Along with the rest of the city, investment in Shaw, LeDroit Park and Bloomingdale started accelerating during this decade. According to the Zillow Home Value Index, the median home price in the zip code 20001 in January 1996 was $138,571, equivalent to $241,596 in 2021, according to the CPI Inflation Calculator.[33] Ten years later, in January 2006, the median had more than tripled, reaching $494,696 (or $671,556 in 2021 dollars).[34] (Prices plateaued during the 2007 housing crisis and for a few years after that during the recovery.)

As my narrators describe in this chapter, row houses in the neighborhood began to shift from serving as investment properties occupied by renters to homes occupied by owners. Many of the vacant homes were purchased by developers or owner-occupants and renovated during this decade.

When prices started rising, some landlords saw an opportunity to sell their properties for a profit, and renters found themselves scrambling for a new home. Often, because of rising prices, these longtime residents were pushed out to cheaper neighborhoods, severing their connections with their community. The displacement so vilified by opponents of gentrification had begun. The city and some residents took note and scrambled to stem the outflow of longtime residents leaving the neighborhood.

MANNA, a nonprofit organization based in Shaw, has been working in the neighborhood since 1982 to keep existing residents in the neighborhood through homeownership. Reverend Jim Dickerson, a pastor with the New Community Church in the middle of Shaw, started the organization by buying crumbling row houses, fixing them up and selling them at a low cost to lower-income buyers.[35] I first encountered Reverend Dickerson in the memoir *S Street Rising* by Ruben Castaneda, a crime reporter who bought crack in Shaw and attended Dickerson's church. The book tells Dickerson's story of settling into the neighborhood in great detail.[36] Later, I brought my children to art classes led by Dickerson's daughter, held in the basement of New Community Church.

According to their website, MANNA's mission is to "help low- and moderate-income persons acquire quality housing, build assets for families through homeownership, revitalize distressed neighborhoods, and preserve racial and ethnic diversity."[37] Over the years, MANNA has led more than 1,200 residents throughout D.C. to homeownership, according to an interview with Robin Lewis, the director of programs and quality control for the Homeownership Center for MANNA. "MANNA wants to help make it possible for people to stay in the neighborhoods that they grew up in, keep them there," said Lewis. "Having done my thesis on gentrification, displacement and affordable housing, I realized that [gentrification] is not something you can just stop. You have to try to get the community to understand. We can develop programs so the community can buy and so that they can stay," said Lewis.

MANNA's development wing works closely with the D.C. Department of Housing and Community Development (DHCD), which subsidizes the cost of building new homes and allows MANNA to sell its units at below the cost of construction.

A recent project in the heart of Shaw, at Eighth and T Streets Northwest, added six new-construction homes to the neighborhood. MANNA was able to sell four of those units at a below-market rate, said Lewis: "They were targeted to people with moderate to low income." Several units were reserved for residents whose income was below 50 percent of the median family income (MFI), while another was held for someone who was making up to 80 percent of the MFI. The process for securing those subsidized homes is somewhat rigorous.

"The people who live there went through a severe vetting process to get those homes," said Lewis. The city has a few other programs, like inclusionary zoning and loans, that are intended to assist lower-income residents buy homes; all of them have long, complex application processes.

Most new developments in Washington, D.C., must set aside some portion of their units for lower-income buyers in a program called "inclusionary zoning." Potential residents take a required class and apply, and the units are awarded through a lottery.[38] DHCD's Home Purchase Assistance Program (HPAP) provides interest-free loans to buyers under a certain income level; the loan repayment is deferred until the owner sells the property.[39]

Right: New Community Church and MANNA, S Street Northwest, 2021. *Shilpi Malinowski.*

Below: MANNA's housing development, Eighth Street and T Streets Northwest, 2021. *Shilpi Malinowski.*

To help residents navigate all these programs, MANNA started the Homebuyers Club in 1985. "Reverend Dickerson realized at the time that people weren't ready to buy," said Lewis. "They had to get credit counselling; they had to get budget counselling; they had to learn how to not only buy but learn how to maintain their credit, how to keep properties so that they wouldn't lose their properties. MANNA has been successful in educating people so that we have a very low foreclosure rate. We help you with your financial stability, with your credit, with your savings, and with your budget. That's where we start. Then we have a one-on-one counselling session with you, we have multiple follow-ups to see where your progress is. We also pull your credit. Essentially, we help people get ready for those programs."

Now, in 2021, said Lewis, "you look at Shaw, there are not many places left to build. For all intents and purposes, Shaw has gentrified, and displacement has occurred."

LEROY THORPE. *We are talking about the 1990s. At the time, I was fighting the convention center, and I told* [my neighbors]: *"Look, gentrification is coming." I bought this house in 1998. I said, "They are building the convention center. What's going to happen is that it's going to be a project that is going to push Black people out of the community. Property values are going to go up; you better get a house right now."*

I would tell those guys, the ones that were being respectful, "Look, man, you guys need to run your [drug] *operation where you are not interfering with people. When you are carrying on all night, morning, evening, you are dropping trash, you are bringing attention to yourself. I don't know what you can do where you can make your business more to where people can coexist. Take the money—buy some properties. Buy the vacant houses, and then you are putting your own Black people in your community." But no one listened to me.*

So, I took my own advice. I bought a house. Gentrification started coming in, because I looked at my numbers as I was running for office. And my numbers were going down in terms of the high percentage points. As the White folks were coming in, my numbers were going down.

I could have done two things—one that went along with the newcomers coming into the community being in the pocket of the developers. Or I could fight for my people to make sure they have housing, jobs—that's what I did. So, that's how I got a reputation of "he's racist, he's looking out for the Black people."

So, White folks were saying, "Who is this brash young man that is bold and talking like Malcom X? He scares the hell out of us." But I wasn't doing nothing against them; I wasn't attacking them for being here. I was saying: "Black people need to have a part of the economics."

Everyone who came before the neighborhood commission, I would grill them—what kind of jobs do you have, are you going to provide jobs for the people?

They thought I was being hostile, but I was looking out for Black people. Black people don't understand how America works—they really don't.

SCOTT ROBERTS. *When I first moved in, this was considered an investment property neighborhood. You didn't actually buy a house and live here. Good God, there were drug dealers everywhere; it was full of crime, and there were homicides going on everywhere—homicides! Who wants to live in a neighborhood full of homicides?*

So, one of the goals that I and some other neighbors came up with was to convert this from an investment property neighborhood into an owner-occupied neighborhood.

In some cases, we would contact real estate speculators and say, "Buy this property." It's better off as a speculator house than a drug house. I want an aggressive real estate person; I want them to look up the owner of record—in some cases they live in Maryland or Virginia—I want them to drive to their house, knock on the door and say, "I have pictures of your house; there are drug dealers there. Here is the list of arrests. Sell the house to me!"

The house at the corner of my blocks was a big blue house; we referred to it as Big Blue. It was a group house; it was a fire trap. We tried to get the fire department to shut it down; they said no. It exceeded maximum occupancy; we tried to get DCRA out there. So, we tried Operation Crackdown, a program with the U.S. Attorney's office. There were a couple homicides there, and there were drug arrests there all the time. The way Operation Crackdown worked is they would go after the property owner and say, "You have a problem property. If you don't do something about it, we're going to seize your property without compensation." Finally, the property owner wakes up.

We would do that kind of stuff.

Then the late 1990s came along; the real estate market came along booming, and then things changed. We weren't necessarily the bargain basement neighborhood anymore.

Mayor Williams was in office then, and one year, they had an event called "Welcome to Washington" at the convention center, and they were

Sixth Street Northwest, 1950s. *Emil A. Press slide collection, D.C. History Center.*

looking for people from different neighborhoods. I was the Bloomingdale person. I was going to stand at a table. Other booths had banners and handouts; I didn't really have anything. This was in the 1990s, before "Here is my QR code." So, I stood at the table, and real estate investors were like, "What have you got?" And I said, "I'm not an investor or broker; I don't have a bunch of properties. I'm just a neighbor—just a dope. I went to Kinkos, and here's a map of the neighborhood."

By that next year, D.C. had been discovered. There was no need to have the same event the next year—what changed was the real estate market.

One day, standing in front of what is now the Providence condo building was a group of Hasidic Jews. I walked up and said, "Hi, I live in the neighborhood. Who are you, and what are you doing here?" They said: "We just bought this house; we are going to renovate it and turn it into condominiums."

And that was the beginning. Then each one of our untenanted apartment buildings in the neighborhood got purchased and was renovated into condos.

GRETCHEN WHARTON. *I'll never forget when the first condo building came on the 1800 block of Fifth Street. It used to be a rent-a-room-by-the-hour place. But it was converted to beautiful condos. And I was talking to*

Houses under construction on New Jersey Avenue Northwest, 2021. *Shilpi Malinowski.*

a woman, a Black woman, who moved in; she said four units are already gone—four law students came and bought condos. I'm thinking, "It's not that easy. But if you are privileged, you're not going to have a problem getting a loan."

Someone was telling me that they were paying $3,500 a month for an apartment. I thought, "I'm going to stay here and fix up my house. I love this neighborhood, and I never plan on leaving here. I don't want to leave Shaw, and the apartments are selling for as much as my house."

MICHELLE CARTHEN. *It started in the late 1990s. It was very clear that the city was not the city that we grew up in. I was raising my kids, and we were busy. We always had after-school activities—we always had football, basketball, Saturday school—all kinds of things that were going on. I couldn't pay attention.*

The houses were being turned into condos. They are being split up. And we are just watching all this happen.

If you were a homeowner, and you could hold onto your house, you did good in terms of wealth. If you got pushed out, it was hard.

Because a lot of those homes were owned by people that lived in them, and they were Black, they worked hard and toiled hard for their properties.

My own thinking is sometimes we just don't teach our kids about generational wealth. It was about the here and now. But this is what you have, this is ours, it belongs to us, let's do what we can to hold onto it and keep it.

GREG MASON. *I had a base station antenna up on my roof on top, a CB radio base station. And I talked all over the world on that radio. I'd sit up there on Fridays when I get off work. I sit in the kitchen, I don't go nowhere, I'm right there. I have all my spaces here—work in the yard, talk on my base station. I might throw a little cookout or something, invite a few of my friends. We just sit here and chill every Friday. This was the meeting place.*

My brother passed. And then my father passed. And then my mother passed. And when my mother passed [in 2000], [some family members] saw a financial window where they can go and just take this from me. I battled with the courts for five years. The next five years were pure hell. I didn't have the money to buy them out.

You know, they didn't care if I was on the street or what; all they thought about was the financial aspects.

The little bit that I got was alright, but it didn't last long because I had to survive. I had to pay bills and stuff, you know, and everything like that.

Because I lived in my SUV that summer until the next summer. It's crazy. I've been struggling ever since—for the last twenty years. No joke. It's crazy how the demons and devils come out when somebody dies.

One night, I slept down where that gas meter is—outside, near that basement right there. I slept down there. I was transporting the physically and mentally disabled children and adults and the dialysis patients also. I'd get off work, and I go to my spot over in Northeast, where we parked the work trucks. I'd sleep over there.

I'd wake up about 5:30 in the morning and get to McDonald's; I'd go in there and wash up. I knew the manager. He said, "Man, look, we know what you went through, what you're going through. It ain't no thing; you can do what you want." In the morning, I go in and freshen up.

The house was paid for. It was paid for. You know, I do home improvement; as far as fixing it up, that wouldn't have been a problem. I was gonna put an octagon window—one that it sits out a little bit—I was gonna put that there. Me and my buddy would take the bricks out and everything.

It bothers me every day what I went through.

A lot of the new people—I know them because I'm always around here. Because I still take care of the rose bushes there in the yard. When the first family moved in here, you know, I met them, and I just kept on taking care of the rose bushes. And then when they left, the other family moved in, and I still took care of the rose bushes. Now, the lady that owns the house now, you know, I still come in and take care of the rose bushes. And that rose bush up against the wall right there, that's the youngest one. That should be about seventy years old.

That was hurtful, and it still hurts. You know, that's why I take care of the yard. When I come in here and work on the rose bushes, I'm at peace.

Greg Mason now lives a few blocks east of his childhood home and maintains a constant presence on his former block. Mason comes by to trim trees and bushes, offer a hand to lifelong friends and meet all the newest faces.

In chapter 7, you will meet the new owners of Mason's former home, Nick Grube and Christina Papanicolaou, who bought the home in 2020 for more than $1 million. Grube and Papanicolaou have a relationship with Mason and complex feelings about how they ended up in that home and what their responsibilities are.

In the 2000s, once crime had calmed down and development started slowly filling in the gaps, new people began moving into the neighborhood. In January 2000, according to Zillow, the average home value was $169,733, or $274,511 in 2021 dollars, according to the CPI inflation calculator.

SCOTT ROBERTS. *By the aughts, stuff was going on, but there wasn't as crazy crime going on everywhere. But nothing was open. If you wanted to go out to eat, you walked to U Street or Brookland or Union Station. There wasn't anything. It wasn't Beirut, but there wasn't anything going on; it was before hipsters.*

John Lucier moved to Shaw from Ohio via Columbia Heights in 2002. His wife, Suki, joined him in 2003. Both work at the Bureau of Labor Statistics. The two can often be spotted biking around Shaw with their elementary-school-aged son, Suki's dyed-purple hair topped by a sticker-covered helmet.

I met Suki a few years ago, when my oldest son enrolled at our neighborhood public school, Seaton Elementary. Suki was always a visible presence at the school—behind a table selling T-shirts or addressing the group at a PTO meeting. In 2018, she became the PTO president.

John and Suki Lucier, 2021. *Shilpi Malinowski.*

JOHN LUCIER. *Of the seventeen houses on the 1700 block of New Jersey Avenue Northwest, there were four houses that were occupied.*

At the time, I lived in Columbia Heights. I'd been living in D.C. for three years, since 1999, and I was turning thirty.

My limit was $300,000.

This area, at that point in time, even $300,000 was starting to be a problem if you wanted any kind of size. In a good neighborhood—forget it. Columbia Heights, it was too late; Adams Morgan, way too late. Those townhouses were already at least a half a million, I couldn't even think about those.

My friend's house east of Columbia Heights was in kind of a gritty area, but it opened my eyes up to "OK, I can live in a gritty area!"

I only had so much money. I also had a roommate, an old high school friend—actually, we had known each other since preschool. He was going to be living with me. I wanted to get a place that had something a little separate. Because I had my friend, there was an in-law suite downstairs, so that way, I had the upper floor, he had the basement, and we could hang out in the middle, and of course, I could afford to pay the mortgage.

I think I looked at four or five houses, and this one was so much bigger and seemed so much nicer.

I paid $310,000—the $10,000 was a little exciting.

I believe someone died in this house, and then the family sold it. It was a Home Depot renovation, and it was definitely move-in ready. I put in an offer that day and told my roommate.

He is six-foot-four, he is 250 pounds, he is half Black, and when he drove by, he said, "You are crazy; we can't live there! What are you talking about?"

And I said, "Well, I put in an offer, so I am moving, dude. I hope you are too!" He came around.

Then Suki moved in, and I was charging her rent, and I didn't charge my roommates rent. So, I didn't pay anything for a while besides utilities. That was pretty cool. Then he left.

There were gambling houses; there were two or three houses with billions of sofas out on the front, just in the yard. I would say, "Hi!" And they would begrudgingly say "hi" to me.

Across the street was much more occupied. There were a lot more people. Across the street, there were two White guys, a couple of White gay couples. They are not worried about the schools as much.

I had some friends come from work, and we were going to the 9:30 Club. We are walking, and we are just up where New Jersey Avenue runs into

Florida Avenue. And the cops zoom up and pull over and say: "What are you doing here?!" And I said: "I live right there." And they were like, "You do?" And even at the time, I was like, "Just you wait." I always felt that this location was just too prime and too near downtown for it not to happen. That's partially why I bought.

But it felt like it might take a long time. I remember Charlie, a guy I worked with, came over, and he said: "You are going to be a millionaire." And I thought "I don't know about that, but I like what you are saying." I'm not a real estate guy; I just needed a place to live, and it worked.

We had some bikes stolen, but basically, things have been great. He used to go to work early in the morning, and he went out, and there were some guys doing a drug deal around his car, and he was like, "Hey, guys, I've got to go to work." And they were like, "OK!" And were very friendly about it.

[My neighbor] Sunny had a lot of people coming and going, and he always kept his eye out for us, and I think that made a pretty big difference. He was always at home, always looking around—out the front, out the back—he had a presence, especially since there were so many empty houses.

SUKI LUCIER. *Sunny would take packages and stuff like that—he was almost like the concierge.*

JOHN LUCIER. *And we had a real rapport with some of the seedier elements, and that helped.*

SUKI LUCIER. *It never really freaked me out. You had to be smart— don't walk around with headphones in, be aware of your surroundings. I always found that looking people in the eye and saying, "Hello," and "How are you doing?" Interacting with people—that basic stuff—that helps a lot.*

Fourth and R was a big drug corner when we first moved here. That was one of the spots. Corner boys out there all the time.

JOHN LUCIER. *And the Valero Gas Station, behind there they were selling a lot. It's still happening, but we are not sure where.*

SUKI LUCIER. *We used to see a lot more overt drug use. There was an empty lot that was a land of broken needles.*

JOHN LUCIER. *When my mom was here, we looked out the window, and someone was shooting up. Maybe it has something to do with the gas station, and that's why there were so many empty spaces on this block.*

I think I understood, since I was a homeowner, that I wanted to be friendly and cordial with people, so I've always gotten along. It's funny because it's really more with the people who have been around, not as much with the new people. It feels a little different. The income levels—if you are going to move in now, with $1 million, versus $300,000, you are making a different kind of income.

SUKI LUCIER. *People started moving in more. Our family who came every few years would say, "Every time I come to your neighborhood, it feels different." It happened pretty quickly.*

JOHN LUCIER. *At the dog park, that is where, all of a sudden, I started seeing more White people.*

John Corea and his husband moved to Bloomingdale in 2002, buying a house backing right into the alley of Crispus Attucks.

JOHN COREA. *I didn't have any sense of where this place was. It felt like a million miles away.*

My husband and I lived in Dupont Circle for a decade before that. We were in a rent-controlled apartment there and missed the whole bubble. By the time we wanted to buy something, we couldn't afford anything over there. So, we started looking around. We wanted to live in LeDroit Park, which is where we thought we bought when we bought this house. They said it was LeDroit Park in the ads! And we didn't realize that it wasn't until after we signed papers. Isn't that funny? It was like, "This place is called Bloomingdale?"

A lot of buildings and houses were empty. The houses that were occupied, a lot of them were halfway houses and things like that. You'd see people around, but they wouldn't talk to you.

And there was a class divide, you know; I was one of the new people coming in.

Predating the farmers' markets at Big Bear, my husband had gotten a grant to do a farmers' market on North Capitol Street and Florida Avenue at a vacant lot.

John Corea, 2021. *Shilpi Malinowski.*

> *Service providers were still there, like the methadone clinic and So Others*
> *Might Eat, which is still there. Homeless people stayed there all day.*
> *The whole focus there was trying to be not fancy—we didn't want the*
> *market to be fancy. It was about trying to get fresh stuff to the neighborhood. It*
> *lasted two summers, and it didn't really get off the ground. People who came*
> *were the African and Caribbean transplants—used to buying in markets.*

Vacant retail spaces and empty alley lots caught the eyes of some of the newer residents—some entrepreneurial residents who imagined public gathering places, restaurants and cafés were able to fill in many spaces with trees, flowers, benches and food over this decade. People had places to gather, sit, picnic and buy a cup of coffee. And once they built it, the people began coming.

The former community center Crispus Attucks, where Michelle Carthen spent so many after-school hours in the 1970s and early 1980s, had been sitting vacant since 1987. In 1990, a fire tore through the building.[40] "It just went down, down, down," remembers Carthen. "Homeless people began living in abandoned vehicles parked on the property, and neighbors complained of drug dealing, prostitution, illegal dumping of construction debris, and other illicit activities in the park," wrote Corea on the official park website.

The geography of the center, located in an alley, created a lot of privacy; because it was off the street, it drew folks who wanted to be free from the prying eyes of pedestrians or those in passing cars. In the 1990s, the privacy concealed illicit behaviors. But could the privacy lend itself to creating an oasis of peace instead?

Corea saw an opportunity to bring a new life to the area.

Starting in the early 2000s, Corea joined a group in reviving the Crispus Attucks Development Corporation (CADC). Throughout the 2000s, the group worked with the city to gain back control of the property and tie up bureaucratic loose ends. Over the next few years, they earned over $100,000 in grants for landscaping projects, resulting in a multiuse space with a green field, meandering stone path, climbing trees and layers of flowering plants that bloom throughout the spring.

Now, the park is almost always in use by someone—a neighbor walking their dog, a mother and child lounging under a tree, a couple sitting on a bench. Children throw frisbees around, groups meet to picnic and celebrate birthdays, readers hang hammocks between the trees and quietly immerse themselves.

Crispus Attucks Park, 2021. *Shilpi Malinowski.*

JOHN COREA. *Before we even bought, when we were looking at the place, we noticed the space back here. It was surrounded by an eight-foot-tall rusted chain link fence, all the way around the entire park. It was not nice looking at all. There was a lot of asphalt throughout a lot of the park, there was a lot more concrete, and at least 50 percent grass or some sort of green.*

During an earlier cleanup, they took the building away. They dumped dirt in the middle. They basically covered up a lot of the rubble and stuff from the old building—they just buried it here. If you go deep enough up, you'll still find the concrete underneath, which makes it difficult to grow things.

Back then, no one came to the park. It was surrounded by a chain-link fence, and it was not nice to be in here. We had to beg people to come in and just hang out in the park to keep it safe.

So, of course, you see a place like that, you are like, "Oh, my god, there's so much, so much potential here for it to be so cool." I kept trying to imagine how it might look like. The model, of course, was Gramercy Park in New York City.

I immediately got involved. I was one of the only White people on the board. The other people on the board, a handful of them were people who were living in the neighborhood for a long time, but most of them were people who were transplants who moved here ten years or fifteen years prior.

I remember feeling very acutely aware that I did not want to be this stereotypical White guy coming in and beautifying Black people out.

The neighborhood had just wrested site control back from the city. They had just taken care of all that legal stuff, back taxes and stuff. It was kind of a perfect time to come in because that was just behind us. And now you start doing beautification projects.

I was also getting involved in other ways in the neighborhood, like with the North Capitol Main Street project. That was a lot to do with beautification stuff, so there was some synergy there. It was easy to connect to the various resources and grant programs.

There was one grant for playground equipment that had already been awarded before I got here. And there ended up being, basically, a lot of NIMBYism. People like things in concept, but they don't want things in their backyard.

There was a lot of concern that there would be a lot of loitering, teenagers smoking dope. They were worried about loitering around playground equipment. Then we wanted to make it into a bona fide basketball court. And the neighbors right back behind it were like, "I don't want that bouncing ball right by my house all hours of the day and night!" Which I can understand. Of course, people are going to be really sensitive about what is right behind their house.

A lot of our efforts early on were about trying to build bridges and being very sensitive to the people who were here for a long time. We had this thing called the Yard Squad, this group of teenagers helping in the park. Originally, we were trying to get them to volunteer and wondered why no one wanted to volunteer. They wanted to get paid! So, we ended up finding money to pay them, mostly out of our own pockets.

There were tons of ideas and many aborted attempts. There were three different grants that we had gotten, and then the kibosh would be put on them.

And also, liability was a big, big thing. Because it's privately owned, it wasn't like the city could be responsible if anything happened back here. So, everyone was really nervous about doing anything official back here, besides passive recreation, which is what you see here.

It's the one thing that everyone could kind of agree on: a green oasis, a place where people could just come, and community could happen.

That's the memory garden; I got that grant, then we ended up getting like more than $100,000 from them over time because the organization [then called the TKF Foundation, now called Nature Sacred] *kept giving us more money because they liked us and we were actually*

Crispus Attucks Park Memory Garden, 2021. *Shilpi Malinowski.*

doing what we said we were going to do. And we raised money, in addition, to match.

Now, I just love it; I think it's wonderful. It's fun that people just adopt it. One day last year, someone had like hung up all these paper lanterns in the memory garden. That was so pretty.

I often wonder what would it be like if I had never gotten involved? Obviously, there were a million people, not just me. But I was at the right place and the right time for that grant, for example. Stuff would have happened anyway, for certain, because people are moving in, and people are starting to like adopt little parts of the park for themselves. What would have happened? At some point, there would have been a Casey Trees event where they planted one hundred trees in the park that one day. And that probably would have happened anyway.

Obviously, this is really valuable land. This could all be condos right now. So, the fact that it's not condos is probably the biggest success. Now, there's a nature conservancy easement on it. It's protected.

MICHELLE CARTHEN. *At some point, we should do a plaque or something for John. He's such a great guy, just a wonderful spirit, just completely selfless. He's just a fixer. He's a wonderful, wonderful person.*

Crispus Attucks Park picnickers, 2021. *Shilpi Malinowski.*

A few blocks down from Crispus Attucks Park, another neighborhood spot was undergoing a transformation. In 2006, Stuart Davenport purchased Big Bear Market, located at the corner of First Street Northwest and R Street Northwest.[41] Davenport spent years tinkering with the space; he served food and coffee and set up tables, turning it into the sort of coffeeshop and restaurant that someone could stop by at any time of day.

He built a pergola out front and began growing grape leaves from it, creating a whimsical ceiling of pluckable grapes. He hired landscapers and built gardens along the edges of the patio. He hung birdhouses from the trees. He hung art from the walls and painted the exterior. He set up Wi-Fi, creating a space for the community to work quietly.

Scott Roberts. *I remember the old Big Bear Market. It was like: you walk in, and you urinate on the floor! You get your Strawberry Hill and came out and sat on the wall. You wiz on the floor inside and wiz on the floor outside. And you see a line of guys sitting here who are totally intoxicated—at 9:00 a.m., you see a line of guys totally intoxicated, smashed for days, lining up to get their alcohol.*

Big Bear Store, 1999. *Steven M. Cummings.*

JOHN LUCIER. *Big Bear brought a lot of changes.*

JOHN COREA. *I felt like development and amenities were going to take forever. And then it ended up kind of hopping, jumping, over Shaw, from Logan Circle to Bloomingdale, when Big Bear opened. That was really a catalyst, Big Bear and the farmers' market there.*

SUKI LUCIER. *Big Bear was a liquor store and then was turning into the café, and the neighborhood fought them tooth and nail getting their liquor license. There had been this liquor store for years, and Sunset Liquor is right across the street.*

That felt like an old neighborhood/new neighborhood fight. And it is a neighborhood gathering place for gentrifiers.

JOHN LUCIER. *There were people drunk as crap in New Jack City* [the playground across the street]. *But then there was "we don't want people drinking wine in a restaurant."*

When Davenport applied for a liquor license for the space in 2010, the divided neighborhood sprang into action. A group of neighbors organized against Davenport and convinced the Area Neighborhood Commission to formally oppose the license, according to a story from the *Washington City Paper*.[42]

As documented in a series by *Washington City Paper* reporter Lydia DePillis, the café became a symbol of all the tensions of gentrification. From one article:

> *"It doesn't matter if it's Black people on a corner drinking beer or whether it is young White folks on the corner drinking wine out of a pretty glass—it doesn't matter who's drinking it, or what it looks like, I don't want it on my block," says Tracey Campfield, who moved to the area in 1998 (and, like nearly all Big Bear detractors, is African American).*
>
> *"I have fought the good fight with drug dealers, and dirty alleys, and rats in the alley, and people drinking on the corners....I don't want to fight that fight again."*
>
> *"A lot of these same old-time residents felt that this was a place in the neighborhood that seemed to be attracting these young White kids,"* [Big Bear cofounder Lana Labermeier] *says. "The Big Bear was blamed for being the cause of it. It was the easiest thing to point to."*[43]

Ultimately, Davenport succeeded in securing his liquor license. The café is still open and serves wine, beer and cocktails. Young White kids do flock to the café, but diversity exists among the regulars there, and Davenport's staff includes both Black and White hipsters; he often pulls in Howard University students to work behind the counter. His favored artist for the café is Steven M. Cummings, a Black D.C.-based photographer whose series "Chocolate City RIP" documents the city from the 1990s and 2000s and who documents honestly what is lost as gentrification spreads throughout Washington, D.C.[44]

To many, Big Bear's opening paved the way for more restaurant and café openings.

JOHN LUCIER. *There were no restaurants. Across the street, there was a seafood place that sold hot dogs and stuff—it was all plexiglass. No Dunkin' Donuts. Obviously, the liquor stores were here, the same ones. You had to go to U Street to get any food.*

This page: Big Bear Café, 2021. *Shilpi Malinowski.*

Above: Commercial strip on Rhode Island Avenue Northwest, 2021. *Shilpi Malinowski.*

Left: Sylvan Theater on Rhode Island Avenue Northwest, mid-1900s. *John P. Wymer photograph collection, D.C. History Center.*

SUKI LUCIER. *Dunkin' Donuts was super early. And Thai X-ing. People lost their minds for that place. It was really good. I think it was really important. There were lines, wait times, the listserv was buzzing, and I think it showed other restaurants that you could have a successful restaurant here. You used to not even be able to get delivery here.*

GRETCHEN WHARTON. *We used to have a lot of corner stores, and they had to survive, but their prices were so much higher than grocery store prices. We didn't have the options. Now that the neighborhood has changed, you can go to several grocery stores or restaurants. My group used to hang out in Georgetown, because that was a safe place to be and had nice restaurants, and I tell them, "I don't have to leave Shaw now! It's all here, finally."*

SUKI LUCIER. *The first time that I walked past a restaurant to get to the restaurant that I was going to, I was like, "Wow." The first time I went to Whole Foods, I came back and was like, "I found where all the White people have been hiding." It was the first time I'd been around that many White people since moving here. It made me feel very weird, like in an alternative universe, going to the Bay Area or Colorado.*

2010s

Housing Prices Triple and Developers Break Ground

When we first moved in, people were selling drugs in front of the house. I went out and offered them cookies and introduced myself.
—*Christina Robbins*

By 2010, Shaw, LeDroit Park and Bloomingdale had attracted the attention of homebuyers across the city. The demographics of 20001 changed visibly between 2000 and 2010; according to census data, the number of White residents jumped up from 1,993 in 2000 to 11,396 in 2010. Though overall population rose by about 6,000, the number of Black residents dropped by over 5,000, to 21,613.[45] In short, between 2000 and 2010 observers could watch a steady stream of White residents moving in and Black residents moving out.

During this decade, the neighborhood experienced explosive growth in home values. At the beginning of the decade, a typical row house here was affordable at a middle-class income level; by the end of the decade, it was not. In 2014, the average home price in Bloomingdale was $556,928, according to data collected by the real estate blog *UrbanTurf*.[46] By 2020, the median home value in Bloomingdale was $882,500.[47]

As property values rose across Shaw, LeDroit Park and Bloomingdale, housing developers saw an opportunity: the steep change over time meant that profits were possible simply by letting time pass. Holding on to a property for a year would yield a profit on its own; adding features that were appealing to buyers, like shiny appliances or a nice slab of marble as the countertop, would drive the profit margin even higher. Developers began scooping up the row houses and collecting hundreds of thousands of dollars in profit upon resale.

In 2015, WAMU 88.5 reporter Martin Austermuhle outlined the practices of one such developer, whose desire to maximize profit resulted in a slew of lawsuits from aggrieved buyers and, eventually, from D.C. attorney general Karl Racine.[48] The developer in question bought and sold dozens of homes in the early 2010s, buying one in nearby Eckington at $280,000 and selling it within a year for $630,000. Upon purchasing and moving in, the homeowner discovered problems that weren't visible during the open house, like leaks in the ceilings, an HVAC system that didn't work and water heaters that didn't serve all the bathrooms.[49] The same developer bought another neighboring home for $280,000, used unlicensed contractors to quickly flip it and sold it within a year for $599,000. That homeowner found rotting wood hidden by a paint job, missing load-bearing walls and beams and a leaky basement. The developer bought and sold homes to up to seventeen homeowners in the area; as the number of unhappy homeowners increased, so did scrutiny from the city.

Eventually, the D.C. Department of Consumer and Regulatory Affairs became wise to the developer. Soon, seventeen homeowners who bought from the developer all received a letter from DCRA's Office of Consumer Protection: "A recent review of agency records revealed potential issues with the presale renovation of your property. It appears that the construction may not have been in full compliance with district laws pertaining to construction, permitting, and construction inspections."[50]

In 2015, D.C. attorney general Karl Racine came down hard on the developer. In the complaint, Racine wrote: "Work was conducted without permits and by unlicensed contractors, and the developer ignored repeated attempts by D.C. regulators that they stop." Racine ordered them to stop selling homes.[51] Eventually, the developer settled with the city and agreed to pay $1.3 million to homeowners.[52]

Not all developers cut corners so dramatically, and many homes in the neighborhood were renovated by the law, with inspections and work that met the safety codes. But the rapaciousness of that story stuck with me.

The quickly rising housing prices in the neighborhood activated their greed. To that developer, that house was a means for generating profit; that was the house's primary purpose. The idea that that house would serve as someone's home became so secondary to the profit motive, the developer didn't even stop to consider what the new owner's experience would be like living in that home, with a leaky skylight, a shower without hot water or a dysfunctional AC.

During this decade, large-scale developers also set their sights on Shaw. JBG Smith, a development firm with over 20 million square feet of real estate assets in their portfolio, according to its company website, has had a large presence in Shaw. It built four residential buildings in the area, adding more than one thousand housing units.[53] "When the Whole Foods opened in 2000, a lot of population migration started occurring," noted Kai Reynolds, chief development officer for JBG Smith. "Having previously lived there, I had always been aware of the charm of the neighborhood, but suddenly, the area was becoming a frequent topic of conversation among my real estate colleagues. The neighborhood is really ideal—you can easily get downtown by public transportation and the many historic design elements, landmarks, and entertainment options are unlike anything you can find in other parts of the city."

Reynolds lived in the area from 2001 until 2006. In part because of Reynolds's familiarity with the area, JBG Smith bid on a large parcel of land in the middle of Shaw that was owned by the Washington Metropolitan Area Transit Authority (WMATA) in 2011. According to the *Washington Business Journal*, JBG paid $10.2 million for the land, which WMATA had been trying to offload for years.[54] Within a few years, the space, which had been home to an empty parking lot and an informal weekend flea market, had become the Shay, a luxury apartment building with a rooftop pool and retailers like a Warby Parker eyeglass store, Compass Coffee and a La Labo perfumerie on the ground level.

A few years later, JBG Smith developed another luxury building in Shaw, dubbed the "Atlantic Plumbing" project. The striking architecture of the building, with a rusty metal exoskeleton encasing glass walls, attracted attention, including some from me. I wrote a piece for the *Washington Post* that wondered if JBG's new building was a part of a movement toward bolder architecture in the city.[55]

To Reynolds, adding housing supply was a benefit to the neighborhood. "The Shay and the Atlantic Plumbing projects were vacant parking lots that were converted into housing supply," said Reynolds. "Nobody was displaced for it, and other housing wasn't taken down. [Creating] housing a block from the metro line is probably the best thing you can do for all kinds of things relative to urban planning policies. The addition of the housing supply has been nothing but a good thing."

The Shay Apartment Complex, 2021. *Shilpi Malinowski.*

In 2018, JBG Smith hired A.J. Jackson as their executive vice-president for social impact investing. Jackson leads the company's effort to preserve housing affordability in neighborhoods, including a project called the "Washington Housing Initiative" that supports workforce housing, or housing for working-class people who make too much to claim eligibility for low-income housing but who can't afford the market prices in the cities where they work. He sometimes encourages JBG Smith to form partnerships with nonprofits like MANNA and has thought deeply about how development firms like JBG Smith interact with other forces of gentrification.

Jackson recognizes the discomfort that some neighbors may feel as gentrification swoops through their neighborhoods. "There could be two things going on simultaneously that can both be true and can feel very different," said Jackson.

One is that you can be adding a lot of new supply to a neighborhood, like Shaw, by building on parking lots. And you can have a lot of rental displacement because people who own row homes that they have been renting out decide that now's a good time either to move back in or to sell the row home and move the tenants out.

> *So, you have these two dynamics occurring concurrently. There's change that's bringing a lot of positive and a lot of investment, but at the same time, you're seeing displacement happen. If you've lived there for thirty years, then two things are happening over the same twenty-four months, it makes for a complex mix and a lot of complicated feelings.*

Untangling these two forces, said Jackson, is made more complex because while new developments tend to attract the attention of the community through publications, or the approvals process that requires developers to seek feedback from the community before getting the go-ahead to start construction, the displacement of renters when owners cash out happens quietly. "You don't put a story in the *Washington Post* when one person sells one row house. So, it can kind of sneak up on the community," said Jackson. "It really gets tricky. There is really no institutional intervention to mitigate that kind of displacement. What is the equitable thing to do when a low-income Black family that's renting a house in Shaw is displaced because the children of the Black family that originally purchased would like to pull the equity out? It's a knot."

In 2021, Reynolds agreed with Robin Lewis of MANNA that the wave of development that was sweeping through the neighborhood had passed: gentrification has occurred. "There's not a tremendous opportunity to add much supply in the neighborhood, and because of historic zoning, it's virtually impossible to take down the existing townhomes in favor of more density. Full build-out is likely close to complete in Shaw," said Reynolds.

In addition to developers, the neighborhood had become buzzy to all sorts of home buyers during this decade. The steep slope of increasing house prices made buying a home feel like a potential investment. Would the prices keep rising? For residents, how did the steep increase in prices impact their relationship with their neighborhoods? If they, as residents, took actions that helped the neighborhood become more and more attractive to buyers, their housing values may increase. It would, presumably, also increase their enjoyment of their home and neighborhood. How did all these forces impact how they interacted with the neighborhood?

MY STORY

This decade is notable for me; I came into the neighborhood with this wave. Though I had been covering Washington, D.C., as a local reporter before, this was when I really began my observations of the neighborhood.

In 2011, my husband and I paid $410,000 for a four-bedroom home, which is divided into two two-bedroom units. It is across the street from the home that was previously owned by the Mason family. We were in our early thirties then, and this was our first and only home purchase—as of 2021, we're still here.

We live in the center of the area described in this book: three blocks from the Shaw Metro Station, three blocks from Big Bear Café and three blocks from LeDroit Park. Our modest home had been owned by the same woman for decades. Rosella had owned several properties on the block for decades and was a landlord to all the tenants; she had begun slowly selling most of them off. Rosella put the property up on the housing market with a single exterior photograph and with one request: that the buyers not evict her downstairs tenant, a single mom.

My husband and I were happy to agree to that. Rosella accepted our offer, which matched her asking price. We kept our downstairs tenant for the next seven years and watched her son grow up. When my husband and I had our first son, our tenant would sometimes bring up books and art materials for him. We made minor improvements to her unit: a new door, an HVAC system. After a couple of improvements, we raised the rent by $150 per month, but we kept it well below the median rent for the neighborhood.

When she told us that she was moving out of the city in 2018, we had a warm goodbye and then invested in improving that unit for our own use. At this point, we had two children and could find ways to use the extra space.

However, we did occupy the upstairs apartment as soon as we bought the house. When Rosella put the house on the market, that unit was being occupied by another single mother. Because we wanted to live there, Rosella told her tenant that she would have to find a new place to live. She was being displaced. After our offer was accepted, Rosella, my husband and I kept pushing our closing date farther and farther into the future as this tenant scrambled to find a new place to live, ultimately closing almost six months after our initial offer. In the end, Rosella helped her tenant; she scanned listings for her, drove her around the city to check places out and helped her apply. She found a place a few miles away. Once her tenant was in another home, we closed on the deal.

I am still unsure of how I feel about that series of events. Though I've now come to understand all of the forces of gentrification and I can see very clearly that my husband and I hold some responsibility for displacing someone out of the neighborhood, I don't think I fully understood that at the time. As A.J. Jackson points out, one of the main drivers of

Shilpi Malinowski, 2021.
T. Jerrod Sharpe.

gentrification displacement is when an owner-landlord sells their house and the renter is pushed out.

But all the forces and potential consequences feel tangled. Washington, D.C., does have a law, the Tenant Opportunity to Purchase Act (TOPA), which gives tenants the first chance to purchase their home if it goes on the market.[56] I know that our seller's previous tenant did receive that chance but couldn't afford it. Was Rosella also responsible? Should she have chosen another buyer who could have continued on as an owner-landlord to both tenants? But Rosella also could have sold the home to a developer who then displaced both tenants, made renovations and then added housing supply at the upper end of the rental market. Were we forgiven because we had at least maintained one unit of affordable rental housing in the neighborhood? Who was responsible? What would have been the most just series of events? These are all questions I'm still trying to answer. But like many other residents who moved in during that time, we were excited to live in the area.

In 2011, we moved into a thumping neighborhood: Big Bear Café was packed with happy caffeinated people, the farmers' market was a Sunday fixture and the sidewalks were busy. This felt like a healthy, exciting neighborhood. We had a vague notion that maybe our home would serve as an investment that would one day appreciate, but we also enjoyed the neighborhood as it was.

I was working as a local reporter in those days, and I quickly became a regular customer at Big Bear Café, writing there, interviewing people, taking meetings and absorbing the atmosphere of the place and the neighborhood. I got to know Stuart Davenport, the enigmatic and visionary owner of the café, as he popped by to grab a drink, investigate the garden and strategize with his store manager about future events they could hold at the space. I often ran into Scott Roberts, a ubiquitous, ever-curious presence who always had a bemused smile and a joke for me.

A few years after we bought our home, Rosella passed away. A single woman with no children and a longtime cat lover who fed the alley cats for years, she was rumored to have bequeathed her entire estate to the Humane Rescue Alliance of D.C.

Over the decade, I watched our block change. The night we moved in, our tenant suggested that we buy a white noise machine, warning us that the drafty windows let in street noise at all hours. As we fell asleep that night, we heard voices chatting, singing and fighting until 3:00 a.m.

When we moved in, the four houses that back up to our alley and face the side of our house were seemingly vacant. Lights never turned on, so it seemed that the homes weren't attached to the utilities; the porches, however, were active. Every night, people gathered on them to talk, drink and sometimes have sex. When we woke up in the mornings, we often saw people asleep there. It was clear that some of them were itinerant folks who were living there. At some point, I looked up the home purchase data; the owners of these homes lived in Maryland. I never met them. The houses remained in that state for years. At one point, one of the homes caught fire; another time, someone desperate to get into a house smashed a window and broke down the door. The ruckus attracted the police, and I watched as they pulled one person after another out of the house and away, never to return. As the years went by, one quiet gentleman was left as the only porch dweller; he slept on the porch every night, often read a newspaper in the mornings and would wave kindly at us whenever we passed.

In 2016, the owners agreed to sell, and it appears that one developer swept through and thoroughly renovated each of the four homes, turning them into eight condos. One by one, each two-bedroom unit was sold in 2018 and 2019 for around $650,000; each of the eight porches we now look out onto are meticulously kept and furnished with matching patio furniture and twinkle lights.[57]

My toughest experience living in the neighborhood occurred in 2016, when my son and I were held up at gunpoint in front of our home.[58] I was unloading my car when a young man pointed a shiny silver gun at my chest and said "Bitch, give me everything." When I told him "I have a child in the car," hesitation passed behind his eyes for a split second. Was he really willing to kill the mother of a toddler for cash and a phone? But he pushed: "Just give me everything." I gave him all my bags, including my phone, my wallet and my son's snacks. The robber ran off and jumped into his van, giddy to realize what he was getting away with. He was a teenager, and his expression reminded me of a kid at an amusement park. As his van peeled away, I noted the license plate number, which I later gave to the police; they tracked down the vehicle and used my phone to track down his apartment building, but for whatever reason, they never arrested him.

That day, I used "Find My Android" to follow the robber's activity; his first stop had been to a known drug dealer a few blocks from my house to buy heroin, crack or PCP. That was the day I learned exactly why it is risky to move into an area with an active drug market.

A few moments after it had happened, while I was standing on the sidewalk in disbelief, shaky, terrified and also enormously relieved that the gunman was gone and the danger was over, Greg Mason walked by, as he often does. I told him everything, and as he handed over his phone so I could call the police, he kept saying, "If I had been there, that wouldn't have happened. I was just here. I should have been here."

After I had my first child, I scaled back my work and spent hours every day out in the neighborhood with my kids. The Shaw Public Library, the parks, the playgrounds and all the neighborhood-serving shops were the scenery of our lives. I got to know hundreds of my neighbors during those years. I learned how the web of community members were all connected.

My next three narrators, Christina Robbins, Ruxandra Pond and Preetha Iyengar, are all mothers of young kids—like me. The parents of this neighborhood are connected through various formal and informal networks, like listservs, a Facebook group, babysitting coops and friendships, and I met these women through these channels.

Christina Robbins and her husband, Brent, moved into Bloomingdale in 2010. She quickly befriended Juan Laster, her neighbor. The two often meet for a glass of wine in Robbins's house after the kids have gone to sleep. The three of us met for this conversation in 2019 in Christina's home.

CHRISTINA ROBBINS. *We purchased our house in early 2010. Our real estate agent said: "I want you to see this house." There was two feet of snow; we had to dig our way into it. We fell in love with it. We knew there were some cosmetic changes that we wanted to do, but we thought, "We can live here." It ended up being a lot more than we anticipated, as every house is, but we loved it.*

When we first moved in, people were selling drugs in front of the house. I went out and offered them cookies and introduced myself.

JUAN LASTER. *I was like, "This White girl is crazy." She is totally out of her mind. I'm not going over there and saying nothing. I was like, "What did you do?"*

CHRISTINA ROBBINS. *I found that they were very friendly—we talked.*

JUAN LASTER. *They were shocked.*

CHRISTINA ROBBINS. *But they stopped selling in front of our house. I think because they realized that this isn't a vacant house anymore; there are neighbors engaging with one another. I'm not criminalizing what they are doing; I'm just going to engage them.*

JUAN LASTER. *"I'm not going to allow you to do this anymore," is basically what she was saying.*

CHRISTINA ROBBINS. *We just thought, "This is all we can afford, and we like the house, and we like the neighborhood." But a lot of our friends thought we were crazy. They thought, "What are you doing?"*

When we bought our house, it had been empty for months. We started to do renovations on our house, and there was an old garage behind the house. We demoed it, I think because it was a sort of a hidden little house and was left open—I think it sat vacant for at least months. We would find needles and condoms—lots of condoms. So, we had to kind of haul that away.

I'm pretty sure my parents were pretty scared, but they are from the Midwest; it's a different culture. But a lot of people now think, "This is such a wonderful neighborhood. I wish we had moved in back then!"

Christina Robbins, 2020.
Shilpi Malinowski.

JUAN LASTER. *Before, I'm not saying that the people weren't interested in getting rid of them, but it does take a certain amount of courage to say, "Look, not here in my neighborhood." It just does.*

One time I saw Brent running across the street, and I thought, "What are you doing?" He saw these two boys running past him with a briefcase. And Brent ran after them in the alley. They ran faster and threw everything out of the way. But that's what you need. You need someone to be vigilant and say: "We are not having that in the neighborhood."

CHRISTINA ROBBINS. *I think it's more effective—not to say that the police aren't wonderful and do a great job, but I think people's first inclination is to call the police. If they see something that scares them, they call the police. But if it's a kid, and if it's something that could be totally harmless, an act of kindness could also dissolve it just as quickly and with less ramifications. I don't want to put people in danger, but I'm not threatening them. I'm engaging and talking to them. I learn something, and they learn something, and it becomes not a dangerous situation. So, I think that can be effective.*

Juan Laster. *I think it's very effective.*

Christina Robbins. *If you talk to people, they are less likely to be angry. If you scream at people, if you threaten people, if you are hostile toward them, it's going to escalate. So, why escalate something that doesn't need to be a problem?*

Sometimes, back here, there were just kids being kids. When there were pop-ups [the creation of a fourth story on top of an existing row house] *happening, and sometimes, the construction equipment wouldn't be locked up, the kids would get their hands on them. One of them was driving a bulldozer, so I went out to talk to them.*

Juan Laster. *She said: "No, no, no. Don't do that."*

Christina Robbins. *Because they don't realize they could knock down someone's whole house!*

Juan Laster. *To them, it was fun, but she went zooming down the alley. I stood right there and watched. I thought, "Let's see how this is going to turn out." I didn't budge; I let her do it.*

Christina Robbins. *These are kids. They are probably preteens. But they can't take hammers and throw them at each other; they can't take sharp objects and break windows. They are just being rambunctious. And it takes someone, any adult, going out and saying: "Alright, guys, let's not do that."*

Juan Laster. *People are more conscious of keeping everything clean and looking decent. Of course, I would see her sweeping out the alley and think, "That's a good idea." So, I started doing it.*

Christina Robbins. *I feel like you don't see as much trash around as you used to. I used to go out there on Saturdays and pick up trash. There used to be gunshots. I would say I heard gunshots more than once. It was more frequent. I never felt like I was going to be shot, but I remember hearing them.*

Juan Laster and Christina Robbins, 2020. *Shilpi Malinowski.*

Juan Laster. *Scott Roberts was so good. There were two guys who were breaking into people's houses, stealing art, and somebody took a picture of one of them, and Scott put it on the email listserv and said: "This is the guy." Within two weeks, they were caught.*

Scott would say, "Hey, there is a robbery. Look out for this guy; he is five feet tall." He would put out a lot of information: "So-and-so had a baby; so-and-so's house was sold for $700,000; they are having a going away party, come on down and say goodbye."

Christina Robbins. *In 2010, we are having a little house party, pre-kid. A lot of our neighbors didn't have kids when they moved in. We just had fun, wanted to meet the neighbors and have a house party because we were all excited that we had a house. Our kitchen, there were holes in the floor; we probably shouldn't have been throwing parties, but we were just so proud and happy.*

We thought we may be here for a couple years. But we fell in love with our neighbors, fell in love with our community; we had kids here. We didn't know we'd have a family here. So, we became engrained in the community. It changed a lot in the last eight years.

I think my kids know all of their neighbors. That's probably true all over the country, but I'm grateful for the fact that I have all of these neighbors, and I like that they are multigenerational. They have Aunty Juan, like a second grandma. They know Miss Mary; they know people of all different age groups and different cultures. They know their friends who live a couple doors down speak French; other neighbors speak German. They are exposed to all this, which I think is wonderful.

People say the neighborhood has changed so much. And it has, but there are still a lot of residents who have been here a long time. Our neighbor next door, Miss Mary, she is ninety-five and has lived here the entire time. She just moved into an apartment that has more assisted living, and her grandson is there, and his mom used to live there. Next to them is the Scotts, and they have been there for fifty years.

The difference in this neighborhood versus others is that we have a lot of houses where the people who owned them still own them. The value has gone up, they have multigenerational families living there, they pass them down to their kids. The property values have gone up, but they are still here.

Juan Laster. *Let me tell you a story. My neighbor Miss Mary—I've been seeing her through my screen door, and I speak to her, and when she got really sick and she had three canes, she still didn't want me to help her pull her garbage can out.*

CHRISTINA ROBBINS. *She is an African American from southern Virginia; she moved to Baltimore during World War II to work.*

JUAN LASTER. *I said, "Miss Mary, just give me a minute; let me come around." But I didn't know that she asked Christina was I an African? Because I used to wear head wraps. All those years that I used to live there. But she never asked me; she asked Christina.*

CHRISTINA ROBBINS. *I thought it was so funny, because they have lived next to each other for decades.*

In 2014, Ruxandra Pond and her late husband moved to LeDroit Park. Pond is the vice-president of Friends of LeDroit Park, a nonprofit organization that supports the park at the center of the neighborhood, which draws in residents with a playground, picnic tables, a wide field and a dog park.

RUXANDRA POND. *We were looking for a place we could afford. We were just starting out as a family. When I walked out onto the deck, I saw this wide-open sky where the park was. So, we both looked at each other. And when I saw that, I was, I thought, sold. We really were attracted by this wide-open sky that you can see from our backyard. It was still at the very top of what we could afford, about $600,000.*

And we go to the park pretty much daily—probably more than once a day. We have our dog. He doesn't like the dog park. He's very shy, but like a little shy guy, but we've walked him in the neighborhood and in the park every day.

So, you kind of start to get to know everything. When we moved down here, my husband, John, noticed the trees weren't doing well. And we are big nature lovers, tree lovers, and just asked the civic association: "How can we get involved to help the trees in our park?" And they said, "Oh, there's a committee on the park." So, basically, that's how we got involved. Within a year, we had organized like a huge tree planting and then watered the trees for the next two summers.

Four or five years ago, we testified [on behalf of the Park at LeDroit] and said, "Here's, like, our deal. Here's our neighborhood. Here's our community, here are all the different challenges that we have." Our park was sort of haphazardly put together after Gage Eckington School closed. It was owned by DMPED, the deputy mayor for economic development. And so, the thinking was that they did kind of a very superficial job because the park was supposed to only be temporary until they figured out how to develop the land/space/lot.

We noticed, for example, a lot of times, the gazebo is used by, say, one family or a couple of people who would want to smoke—smoke pot, frankly—or do a little grilling. And that would kind of push out everyone else who might want to maybe also use that seating area, because that seating was just so close together. So, we wanted to stretch it out and really allow people space.

One of the Friends of the Park's priorities was to get DPR, the Department of Parks and Recreation, to take this property on in order to ensure the park would not be redeveloped. And I don't recall the mechanics of it, but basically, at some point, we succeeded. Somehow, we succeeded. So, now, it's a DPR property.

We took a survey of the community, asking what would they want improved with the park, and the main priorities were: the field, shade, safety, movement of people. The council members put money in the budget; it was passed. And we had one batch of renovations last year and then another second round this year.

The first set of renovations was to redo this field and soil that would allow for grass to grow and for trees to grow. Then this round is putting in shade over the two playgrounds.

We're also getting a splash pad, which we think is really important. You may have noticed, kids would come and pull the hose out of the community garden and splash around—as kids do. So, we think that will really, really help.

The splash pad is surrounded by three kinds of curvilinear seating structures, because we think that there's no good space right now for community members to gather in a communal way. So, these three benches are roughly aligned in a circle, so people could have a small community meeting or story hour or just chat. We wanted to create a space for, basically, gathering.

John and a couple other people watered that first batch of trees for two summers, and we got to know a lot of people that way. Sometimes, the little kids would come help. Since I've been so involved, it's really—I'm not exaggerating—made my heart soar to see how many people use this park since the virus hit. People working out, people picnicking—now that we have this field that you can actually use. Lots of kids would play pick-up football

Ruxandra Pond, 2021. *Shilpi Malinowski.*

and soccer and Frisbee. There were people coming in that I had never seen, like, young guys, who would come and just play soccer here. Lots of working out and little kids practicing various activities, dogs, people with their dogs. Over the summer, there was a lot of socially distanced socializing—everyone on their little blankets, six feet away. It just really made me happy to see that.

This was a place that lots of people could use. Of course, once, we were here in the gazebo, trying to have a small family meal outside. And we had to duck for cover because we heard gunshots. I've been on a long email chain; every time there's gunshots, I reply to all the same folks—the council member, the ANC, the district commander, his lieutenant and a couple of neighbors. The council member and the police, they're always talking about violence interruption and gun recoveries.

These activities are happening so close to the park, and I would say two, three, four times a year, every year, there's been shootings across the park or right on V Street, Elm Street or U Street.

When we talked about designing, redesigning the shade and the splash pad and seating, we were always cognizant of sightlines. We really don't want anyone to be able to hide, and we just want people to feel much safer being able to see right across.

For community members and the Friends of the Park, our theory is that the more we make the park welcoming for all kinds of users, during all parts of the day and the year, that will help make it safer. Because more and more people are around, it hopefully pushes out illegal activity or questionable activity. I don't know—maybe that's not true. But we've been pushing for these renovations partly with that in mind.

I think it's worked out. We think that maybe some of the people smoking pot had nowhere else to go. So, maybe if they move further away from the playgrounds to the newly installed seating, they have somewhere to sit now and then the kids could still play without breathing in pot smoke, because parents would complain.

Juan Laster. *I have a garden that I won in a lottery, next to Common Good City Farm, near LeDroit Park. I won it, and I love it. You go there, and you meet a lot of people. We have a farmers' market. If I miss a farmers' market, it's like a missed dinner. It's a social gathering. We swap recipes. People say: "What's chard?" And I'm like, "You don't know what chard is?" And then someone has spinach or a strange-looking fruit, and he'll tell everybody what to do with it and how he cooks it. If I miss a Wednesday over there, my whole week is off.*

LeDroit Park playground, 2021. *Shilpi Malinowski.*

> *Someone I met who was pregnant, she had a baby, then she brought her*
> *baby there. I see Scott Roberts there every Wednesday. He snaps pictures*
> *for his blog. And the Common Good City Farm, they also have a CSA for*
> *people who are interested in their vegetables.*

Preetha Iyengar and her husband moved to Bloomingdale in 2016, while Preetha was pregnant with their first child. Preetha is Indian American, and her husband is from the Czech Republic. They often share their home with Preetha's parents, who helped care for their children during their infancy. While we talked, Preetha's mother, wearing her long hair in a braid and dressed in a sari, played with the children.

By the time Preetha started looking for a home in the area, bidding wars were common.

> PREETHA IYENGAR. *I don't know if a lot of neighborhoods are like this*
> *now, but we know ten families on these two blocks of Seaton Place Northwest.*
> *We bought this house from a Black family, and they were just retiring*
> *and moving to Florida.*
> *We put an offer on another house down the street and got outbid, and we*
> *saw this house. They had a contract, but the sale had fallen through. They*

Preetha Iyengar, 2021. *Shilpi Malinowski.*

listed it on Thursday and took offers on Monday. It was on the market for four days, and we had learned the lesson from a previous offer that we lost, and we had a higher ceiling and did it quickly.

The way we got this house—and I honestly think if we had waited a year, we wouldn't have been able to buy an entire house. So, we got in right when we could.

When we moved, we didn't want to move to somewhere like Upper Northwest—we wanted a more diverse neighborhood. That's why it also appealed to us to come here specifically. And we used to come to Boundary Stone a lot before we moved to the neighborhood. So, we were happy there was a commercial strip near the house. Also, it was central enough that you could walk everywhere, but you could get an actual three-bedroom house, a good-sized house. We wanted to live really centrally in D.C., to be able to walk to our workplaces or live within a twenty-minute commute within our workplaces. It felt like a house we could stay in for a while.

We met so many neighbors because of little kids, from being outside with the kids. And our neighbor next door is an older woman in her seventies, and she has been here for a long time. I think she was in that house with her parents, and she is lovely. When we moved here, there weren't too many vacant houses—maybe, like, two houses.

My parents have been with us twice for a year helping with the kids. And they are very friendly and spend a lot of time outside with the kids. And half the time, people would meet my parents, and we would come home from work, and they would be outside talking.

Most of the people I know have been here for eight years or less. And they are younger, and they are having kids. I think we are very lucky to live somewhere where I just walk around and see people I know on almost every block. I very rarely can walk from point A to point B without seeing someone that we know and, most of the time, someone we are actually friends with. That is amazing. We really value that a lot.

And people having babies—that must be a huge indication of safety. Nothing has directly happened to us except for packages being stolen, but that happens everywhere.

Our neighbor behind us makes our backyard view look so nice—a willow and wisteria to sit and look at.

6

2020

Porsches, Millionaires and Black Lives Matter

In my mind, gentrification is a lot like colonization. You are taking away the land and resources from native communities. We paid a lot of money to live here, and most people can't afford it. So, I guess that's where the guilt comes in.
—Christina Papanicolaou

By 2020, many Bloomingdale, Shaw and LeDroit Park row houses were selling for well above $1 million. In early 2021, a four-bedroom home in Shaw sold for $1.6 million, a six-bedroom home in LeDroit Park sold for $1,925,000 and a four-bedroom home in Bloomingdale sold for $1,630,000.[59] In 2018, according to the *Washington Post*, the median home sale price in 20001 was $817,000.[60]

Both the overall population and the proportion of White residents has risen since 2010. According to estimates from the census, the population of the zip code 20001 in 2020 was 52,621, an increase of more than 10,000 since 2010. The number of White residents rose by more than 12,000, to 23,532. The number of Black residents fell by about 2,000, to 19,465. For the first time in 70 years, White residents now outnumber Black residents.

The neighborhood can't really be called an investment neighborhood anymore; the newest buyers have dropped their expectations that their investment is likely to grow.

SCOTT ROBERTS. *Right now, it's a seller's market—you buy what's available, you don't do your homework, I get it. We also transitioned from*

LeDroit Park home for sale, 2021. *Shilpi Malinowski.*

a starter house to a nonstarter house. No one is spending $1.3 million on a row house as a starter row house.

GRETCHEN WHARTON. *The house right up the street, on the 1800 block, with an elevator, sold for close to $1.7 million. It is mind blowing.*

CHRISTINA ROBBINS. *It is funny, there was also a boardinghouse on the block, and the cops would always come there, and there would be fights out front and sometimes nudity in the front. This was 2010, 2011. That house, one of the guys who owned it had personal issues, and the house was going downhill, and people were inhabiting the house and selling drugs there. So, then he sold it, but he is still in the neighborhood; we still see him around.*

A builder came and flipped it, turned it into a pop-up. And when the new people moved in, people kept saying, "Did you know your house used to be a crack house?" They turned it into two beautiful homes. One was almost $1 million, the other was $700,000; it was crazy. They moved from Bethesda to buy the crack house. We were just like, "Are you kidding me?"

MICHELLE CARTHEN. *The White people, they moved in for the wealth. They want to buy the house and want to sit on it for a year or two. And then, "I'm going to leave." They haven't stayed. They go inside for the winter; they come out with a baby. Two years later, at the time the baby gets ready to go to school, they are gone.*

That's exactly what I saw. They don't really talk; they don't really speak to us. A long time ago, if you moved into the neighborhood, you walked over, you introduced yourself. They don't do that. And that's kind of sad. And it creates a sense of "I just live here."

SCOTT ROBERTS. *The community has totally transitioned. When I moved in, my block was working-class. People worked in the dairy, worked in the factory, worked in the garage. They had low-level government jobs, federal or D.C. jobs, mostly Black people. Now, the people who are moving in are mostly attorneys, professionals. I have two households on my block who have live-in au pairs. That is telling. I feel like I should be cleaning the toilets of some of my neighbors, really. I am the working-class guy, the poor Irish guy. We all have the same house, but people buying a half house for $850,000 or up to a $1 million for a half house condo, it's like, "Really?"*

SUKI LUCIER. *At the city council hearings for Shaw Middle School, someone said: "Everyone in Shaw is a millionaire, so they have options." That feels completely incorrect, but then you think about the equity. People think you must have money. So, now, I find myself always slipping into the conversation when we moved here as a way to say, "I'm not a rich person." At a certain point, there is almost a negative connotation—that you are part of the group that is gentrifying and displacing.*

The assumptions are very interesting, especially the assumptions that people make based on your neighborhood and how that changes as your neighborhood changes and how people perceived us. Before it was like, "OK, you are risk takers." For people who were here, they were like, "OK, they are cool, they are down with the neighborhood!" Over time, it was like, "OK, you must be wealthy to live there."

SCOTT ROBERTS. *One owner of a local market at Second Street and Rhode Island Avenue Northwest told me he noticed as people were changing demographics. Before, neighbors would prepare their meals at home—they would come in and buy a leg of lamb or a whole turkey and they would cook it. And then the demographics of the residents changed. How did they change? The neighbors were looking for more prepared foods. Like, "I'm too lazy to cook. I'm not really going to do a Thanksgiving Day–style roast.*

I'm not doing that." And he got ticked off. He got mad at people coming in and wanting to buy an ice cream. This is just carbohydrates. This is candy. And he had high-end chocolates, but it was just below him. He got ticked off that people didn't want to buy whole chickens.

All the retail spaces, when they were purchased, they had to be renovated from the ground up—electric, entire gutting, everything. In the old days, every time there was a turnover, it took a year and a half. Now, they already have a working floor, a working kitchen, maybe it came with a liquor license, a kitchen that already passed the D.C. Department of Health inspections. That kind of stuff—the turnover is totally different. Rustic Tavern was there, then Tyber Creek moved into that space, did it take her a year and a half? No, she was open in six months or less.

JOHN LUCIER. *All the houses are occupied now. Most of them have been popped back, a couple have been popped up, a lot of them have had basement renovations, and some added stories and made them into two-unit condos.*

What does it feel like to buy one of these homes now?

Meet Nick Grube and Christina Papanicolaou. The couple, hip thirty-somethings, bought Greg Mason's old home in 2020, after renting in the neighborhood for two years. Like the Masons decades ago, they can often be found sitting in their side yard, chatting with everyone who walks by—Grube, with his long locks and in his constant rotation of Hawaiian shirts from his home state, and Papanicolaou, with her vintage clothing and New York City style. Grube is a journalist working for a Hawaii-based publication, and Papanicolaou is an artist and arts administrator.

I met Nick and Christina when they rented a house next door to mine. During the 2020 pandemic, when we were all grounded and homebound, we started seeing each other all throughout the day. Our backyards shared a giant maple tree, and my sons would throw sticks to their dog through the gaps in the fence while we chatted. We would all find ourselves sitting on our front stoops in the evenings, processing the pandemic. Both Christina and I lost parents that year, and we formed a deep connection through our grief.

Later, in May and June, we watched Black Lives Matter protests march right in front of our homes. The protests spurred many conversations about the neighborhood and gentrification, as we marveled at sights like a neighbor's Porsche parked on the street and a house on the block selling within days for $1.3 million.

Nick Grube
and Christina
Papanicolaou, 2021.
Shilpi Malinowski.

The events of that summer seemed to shake up the racial dynamics of our neighborhood in ways that I'm still trying to understand. Black Lives Matter (BLM) signs are ubiquitous throughout the area—while, at the same time, the proportion of Black residents drops. But within a still very segregated Washington, D.C., our gentrified neighborhoods are the rare places where White people and Black people do live alongside each other in significant numbers. In our neighborhood, White people with BLM signs in their yards actually had an opportunity to put their declared beliefs into practice with their neighbors. What would they do? Would they break out of racially uniform social groups and start forming friendships across race? Would they choose to send their White children to a majority-minority school, rather than a charter school or private school with a higher percentage of White children? Would they shop at Black-owned businesses?

George Floyd protest down Fourth Street Northwest, 2020. *Shilpi Malinowski.*

I think, among other things, the summer of 2020 led us to consider how our decisions impact the collective. What is our responsibility to each other? How do all our individual decisions impact the dynamics of our whole society?

I could feel a subtle shift in the conversations that happened postprotests; people were more willing to grapple honestly with how race plays a part in their decisions.

It is within this atmosphere that I sat with Grube and Papanicolaou for their interview, which took place in their home in early 2021.

> NICK GRUBE. *My mom was out here most of my life, so I had familiarity with this neighborhood in the 1990s. Shaw was not a place I would have ever gone to back then.*
>
> *In 2018, I had a few days to find a house because I was out here for my job.*

Black Lives Matter lawn sign in Bloomingdale yard, 2021. *Shilpi Malinowski.*

Christina Papanicolaou. *So, we got an Airbnb in Shaw.*

Nick Grube. *She walked around the Airbnb neighborhood, and she said, "Oh, it's great. There's stuff around here! Grocery stores, restaurants, Calabash."*

Christina Papanicolaou. *My first encounter with D.C. was a Calabash* [a neighborhood tea shop] *experience. I was coming from living in New York for twelve years and Brooklyn for eight years. I was used to the convenience of city life and just having a little corner store nearby. So, when I was around Shaw, I thought, "Oh, all right. I can do this!"*

Nick Grube. *It was convenient for work and near the train, which was important to the New Yorker. It was near urban commercial centers and felt a little bit like a Brooklyn-y area.*

Christina Papanicolaou. *Living in Brooklyn, you know about gentrification, but there are so many transplants. There are so many people not from New York in New York. And there's so much happening that gentrification is not on your mind.*

But in D.C., I felt it right away. I mean, it's so obvious. You see these old row houses and you get a sense of who the local community is. And it's just so stark when you see a developed house or condo. And just the people that are so clearly not from here.

I mean, it's just very black-and-white to me.

With the intimacy of D.C. streets, in comparison to New York, where you kind of just look forward and walk, here, I feel like you have to engage with the person you walk by just out of respect. I mean, we all live so close to one another.

NICK GRUBE. *Let me give you an anecdote. When we were looking for houses, we went to Seaton Place, because I was looking on Craigslist for places, and everybody kept talking about Big Bear Café like this was some sort of magical place. Like, who cares? It's a coffee shop? That's how I thought of it, anyway.*

The apartment was over near Bacio [a pizza restaurant in Bloomingdale].

So, we look at this English basement on Seaton Place Northwest. And we liked it. I mean, it seemed nice enough. The landlords, a White couple, seemed nice enough, had a baby.

I was asking, "What's this neighborhood like?" Because D.C. is not always bustling. In this neighborhood, some days, there won't be many people on the streets. And that was one of those days.

Then they said: "Oh, Bacio is great, blah, blah, blah." But then, the person who could have been my landlord was talking about when he and his wife moved there, and they described themselves as "pioneers."

And that term just struck me as a bit funny and also said a lot about what he meant by that. He's a White dude moving into a Black neighborhood that probably really had some issues with crime or whatever. I just remember that felt so funny to me.

What did pioneers do? They moved west and helped eradicate Indians.

CHRISTINA PAPANICOLAOU. *We're definitely hyperaware that we're gentrifiers. And I would say I'm very self-conscious about it.*

In my mind, gentrification is a lot like colonization. You are taking away the land and resources from native communities. And in doing that, you are depleting the culture of what was originally here. And that's why I feel guilty. I'm just this person coming from the north and taking away from someone that has strong ties to this house. But it would have been somebody else if it wasn't me.

We paid a lot of money to live here, and most people can't afford it. So, I guess that's where the guilt comes in.

What are we supposed to do? Are we just supposed to stay put and never leave where we're from?

Nick Grube. *You are kind of damned if you do, damned if you don't. Let's say, as a gentrifier, you go and move to a neighborhood that's already been gentrified, and you pay that exorbitant rent. All you're doing is reinforcing a system of exorbitantly high rents that have already forced people out and are keeping people forced out. You're pushing for more segregation by doing that or staying put.*

I think you can be a good neighbor. Look people in the eyes. Say hello.

Christina Papanicolaou. *I guess the solution is just to be respectful to the people that live here and that are originally from here. How can we give back in some kind of way—or at least shop with local businesses? And I don't know, support local music or culture? I don't know. Do we give mutual aid donations? I don't know!*

We are very aware of our circumstances.

Nick Grube. *People tend to go to where they can afford to live. And, you know, in our case, we're not flippers. We're not coming in to flip a house. We're not trying to make a profit.*

I have an anecdote. Our first rental was an English basement in LeDroit Park, and our landlord was a Black woman from D.C. She was awesome. She wanted to have a reliable tenant that she could trust, and it was under market value.

The landlord got sick. She had cancer, and she wanted to sell the house to help pay for the treatment. Once the for-sale notices went out, developers were showing up! All these White people knocking on my door asking us about our TOPA rights. "Don't lose your TOPA rights," they told us.

I had first right of refusal to buy the house, and developers would come to the renters and try to work them into cutting a deal with them. [The developers] wanted to hold [the owner] hostage so that they would have first right of refusal to buy the property so they could turn it into a condo.

It was so shady. TOPA is all about not being able to kick a current tenant out; it's a strong tenants-rights city. But it was being used to complicate the potential of closing, because they can hold up the sale.

We're looked at like fresh meat; there's blood in the water. Developers were writing our names down, sticking stuff in the door, handwritten notes, saying, "Call us, call us!" We didn't want to do anything to hurt [our landlady].

Grube and Papanicolaou know Mason's history in the house, and the three are friendly. Mason is often coming by to chat with them, to do some landscaping or to send a warm text to Christina as she was grieving her mother.

CHRISTINA PAPANICOLAOU. *Mr. Mason maintains a relationship with everyone that steps foot in this house. He came over today and was talking about the roses that his mother planted. He's going to come over this week and trim one of the trees because it's engulfing another tree on the sidewalk. So, he said, "I'm going to come in with my clippers." He's super nice.*

It's one of the reasons why we fell in love with this house. We can feel the energy of the Masons in here, for sure. We still get [his mother's] *mail. I just want to be respectful to Mr. Mason.*

He should have had the right to live here. He should have been able to hang on to it, and he should have had the choice whether he wanted to sell it or not for however much he wanted.

NICK GRUBE. *It's just an unfortunate family situation. I think, when people die, it's bad. It's crazy. Mr. Mason is a part of this house and was a part of our discussion when we were buying the house. And having him take care of the rose bushes—these are things that we actually considered when we look at our house. If we do landscaping, the rose bushes don't get touched.*

CHRISTINA PAPANICOLAOU. *They are eighty years old, those roses. It's incredible. And they're strong; they bloom every year. And we made a vow to each other; we're leaving the rose bushes.*

NICK GRUBE. *We cherish Mr. Mason in a way. So, once, we were out of town, and Mr. Mason was here tending to the yard.*

CHRISTINA PAPANICOLAOU. *He was just trimming his mom's rose bushes, and this woman steps onto the property. She was concerned about the stray cat under the stairs; this cat that's lived on this property for fifteen years. She was a newbie. This girl was so entitled that she walked onto the property.*

Nick Grube. *He asked her, "Excuse me, miss, what are you doing here? This isn't your house." And she was like, "It's not yours either!" And starts yelling at him and treating him like fucking garbage.*

Later, I asked him: "What did she say?" He didn't feel comfortable telling me, and to me, that entire situation became infuriating.

Because not only is this guy part of the community and for that woman to be disrespectful to him on property that was his but is now ours....He had explicit permission from us to be at the house. But the way she acted made it seem like he was the one who was out of place in that situation.

Greg Mason. *This* [house] *was ground zero for me. Yeah. You know, that's why I'm always around here.*

Part II

LIFE IN AN INTEGRATED NEIGHBORHOOD TODAY

7

PRESENT DAY

Families, Playgrounds and Schools

It's made me, at a fundamental level, question this whole thing of "I just want what's best for my child." I also think we've kind of been sold this lie that there's a solution to the racial problem where everybody benefits. We want it to be a win-win situation, where everybody comes out better than we are now. And I don't think that's realistic. I don't—I think they have to give something. And that's scary. That's an investment. And that's radical.
—*Suki Lucier*

Families fill the blocks now. Playgrounds have been fixed up and are in use; overall, school enrollment at Seaton Elementary School in Shaw and Langley Elementary in Bloomingdale increase year after year, as does the proportion of White students.[61]

SCOTT ROBERTS. *Back when there was a spa—Sol Day Spa and Salon—when I found out a woman in the neighborhood was pregnant, I would buy her a spa gift certificate. Then there was a baby boom, and I thought, "OK, this is getting kind of expensive."*

So, now, I go to open houses; I can spot them a mile away and I say, "So, you're thinking of buying in the neighborhood?" They say, "Yeah!" Double income, no kids…and I say, "No kids, right? Here's what will happen—when you move to this neighborhood, you're having your first kid. That's going to happen. You move in here, you buy your house, you have your first kid here." They say: "We are?" I say, "Yes. If you're not ready

Kennedy Recreation Center, 1950s. *Emil A. Press slide collection, D.C. History Center.*

Kennedy Recreation Center, 2021. *Shilpi Malinowski.*

for that, don't move to this neighborhood. That's guaranteed. There is more in the water than lead. They put a fertility element in the water."

At first, DINKS moved in, they have a kid, the kid hits three or four or five, and they are out. Without a doubt, they leave. Then the neighborhood starts transitioning; the first kid hits six or seven, and there is no real estate sign in the front yard.

Another sign—White woman by herself with a baby carriage walking around by herself after dark. You see that, and you go, "Holy crap." Really. Holy crap.

In 2016, I enrolled my then-three-year-old son at our neighborhood school, Seaton Elementary. Like the neighborhood, the school is gentrifying; every year, the percentage of White children increases. In 2016, the racial demographic makeup of my son's Pre-K-3 class was evenly balanced between Black, White, Asian and Latino children. In the year that he enrolled, the proportion of White students at the whole school was 10 percent, according to enrollment information from DCPS. In 2019, his younger brother joined him; by that year, White kids made up 14 percent of the total student body, and his Pre-K-3 grade was about 50 percent White.[62]

Seaton Elementary School, 2021. *Shilpi Malinowski.*

The diversity went beyond what was visible through demographic data. Several children were exposed to English for the first time in that classroom, while others were the children of second-generation immigrants who spoke fluent English. The economic makeup was more hidden and did not track with race; parents quietly scanned each other and discovered through conversations at drop-off and pick-up who has similar educational and professional backgrounds. Upper-income parents existed in all racial groups.

The school, as a whole, was designated as Title 1, with more than 40 percent of the students coming from low-income homes. The school explicitly supported the various language groups, hiring staff with fluency in Spanish and Mandarin to act as liaisons between those communities and the administration. For a while, I attended a monthly parent breakfast meeting with a staff member who was bilingual in Spanish and English; the dozen or so parents who attended spoke in a circle about our experiences with the school, and the staffer translated so that everyone could understand. All of the official school and PTO communication—emails, flyers—were translated into English, Spanish and Mandarin.

People of the same race often clustered together. The PTO meetings were packed with White parents, and the leadership of the organization was overwhelmingly made up of White moms with a couple of Black parents. Latino families could be seen chatting with each other during drop-off and pick-up, and the Mandarin-speaking community communicated with each other via WeChat.

For many parents, this was our first time being in such an integrated environment. How do we do it? How can we be a cohesive community with so much racial, economic and language diversity? I was deeply curious about the dynamics at play.

As a relatively privileged South Asian American, I held an interesting role. Throughout my school and work life, I have often been a racial minority in majority-White spaces. I was very used to navigating those spaces. At the same time, I am the child of immigrants and feel huge amounts of tenderness, empathy and similarity with immigrants who are putting their kids in the public school system as a path to success.

For me, the diversity of the school was a huge plus. My husband is White, and my children are both the color of milky tea, with brown hair and dark eyes. In some situations, they are wholly accepted in White social groups; in other situations, I have seen them othered and excluded. At this school, they are never othered in their classes; with no majority race, all of the kids are free to be individuals.

I know that as both of my sons grow up, they will feel that tension: do they disappear into their passably White appearance and reap the benefits of that White privilege? Can they be proud of their Indian identities and bring that with them? Will our society change quickly enough so that self-hatred about their brownness will never be an issue?

At his school, my son has daily practice in seeing people of all races as individuals. Picking him up, I would often find him running around in a group with a Black child, an Asian child and a Latino child. And academically, he was being judged as an individual at Seaton and not being pigeonholed in any way based on his race, and he was seeing kids of all races succeed. I hope their experience at the school makes them less likely to develop racial stereotypes as they grow up.

In Washington, D.C., school choice complicates our decisions. Because of the school lottery system, children have the opportunity to try for spots at charter schools or other D.C. neighborhood schools. The high housing prices in our neighborhood also mean that parents can easily move into other school zones to seek exactly the experience they want. Instead of opting for the default neighborhood school, many parents feel compelled to optimize their child's school experience. But how can you really judge schools? Comparing curriculum, teachers and facilities seems like the fairest way to assess the quality. What about the demographics? Did parents want their children to have peers in the same racial group?

In 2017, I joined the PTO board and played a small role in organizing events, like monthly coffees and parties in the garden. In board meetings, I felt the undercurrent of two themes creating the subtext of many discussions: one, how do we make this school desirable to as many people as possible so that people opt in and enroll, and two, how do we make sure that every child is included and feels equal? The first question often led the group to attempt to make the school attractive to upper-income White families; the second question dealt with how to make sure that didn't lead to a hierarchical environment.

The most heated discussions I observed happened when those two currents came into conflict with each other. For example: what happens after school? At some public schools in upper-income areas, parents pay for extracurricular activities, like karate, ballet and robotics clubs. At Seaton, there were parents with means who were eager to pay for those activities for their children. But the majority of the children would not be able to afford it, so they would be excluded in a very visible manner.

When I first entered that school, we had a principal who was completely opposed to any tiered systems. We are a community, she felt, and all the

This page: Shaw Library, 2021. *Shilpi Malinowski.*

children need to feel as though they are part of the same community, with the same opportunities. A pay-to-play option would have been corrosive to that feeling. Many people agreed, and the paid extracurricular activities never took hold at Seaton.

For many families with two working parents, after-school activities are huge considerations. They wanted that time to be valuable. And every year, my older son's class at Seaton lost upper-income families to other schools and neighborhoods—some explicitly because of the humble after-school offerings.

GRETCHEN WHARTON. *I love the fact that multiethnic people live here. I love the fact that they have children and babies—I've been to so many first baby showers. I love that—the energy and the families. I don't see a lot of teenagers, but there are young parents with babies. I kept thinking that my mother would roll over in her grave if she looked out her window and saw a young Caucasian woman walking down the street, rolling her baby carriage and walking her dog. Nobody in that era would have imagined that it could happen, but I think it's wonderful.*

SUKI LUCIER. *The best part of the gentrification of Shaw has been the families coming back. We have a neighbor who has lived here forever, and we were out back in Richardson Place, playing baseball and having fun, and he came up and was like, "This makes me so happy. I grew up here, and that's what it was like—kids running around on roller skates, making noise. It's so nice to see that again."*

JOHN LUCIER. *The playground on Florida Avenue, we used to call it "New Jack City." It was very scary. People lived there; it was all dark. How much better must it be to live right next to it now.*

CHRISTINA ROBBINS. *Every other house, if not more on this street, has a baby—on both sides.*

JUAN LASTER. *I like it. I think hearing the kids screaming and yelling and running all over the place—it doesn't bother me. I grew up with a big family. My sister had eight kids. I like to hear the laughter and the screaming and the yelling, like when [Christina]'s daughter and Olivia see each other, they are like, "Aaahhhhhh!" They scream to the top of their lungs. They talk to each other two houses over. I think it is more interaction now. Kids bring people out of the house.*

Florida Avenue playground, 2021. *Shilpi Malinowski.*

Suki Lucier. *In 2013, once the boundary changed* [with more of Shaw in bounds for Seaton Elementary School], *the boundary really made the neighborhood. Having a higher performing school be the option, people opted in, and they were active people who made it a better school. The boundary helped encapsulate the neighborhood. And it gave another excuse for families to know each other and interact. Little things, like running into people you know at events, is so nice and centering.*

We all make tradeoffs, so for me, I always assumed one of the tradeoffs would be not having as cohesive a neighborhood feel as in a suburb or small town. It did feel that way for a while, but having children ties you into your community. The library was huge for us when he was a baby—and how you meet people in the public spaces. It did change things a lot. It's so much more now than what I expected. Dropping my kid off with a neighbor for a minute or running out of this or that....I have people to call on.

When you try to stabilize a dune and the grasses are interconnected and provide a stabilizing force, I think that's what families do to a neighborhood. Because you connect to each other through schools, and it builds those roots that help it hold on.

SCOTT ROBERTS. *So, there is a whole discussion about "where do you send our kids to school?" But then the charter school movement came along. So, then there is the whole schism between public school and charter school, and then the whole charter school idea scattered people to the winds. Some of the neighbors go to DCPS, some go to charters....It's all separated.*

But more and more people are piling into DCPS. One of our neighbors who was White, he and his wife had two daughters who were White, and he sent his kids to Seaton. And they were the only White kids in the school. So, whenever there was a school tour, guess who was always on the tour? Those two White girls. I heard that from more than one source. Even one of the teachers there said, "We have two students who are always on the school tour."

PREETHA IYENGAR. *Langley is good; it's our neighborhood school. We did look at schools a little bit just to see what would be OK in five years or three years. When we moved in, I was thirty-eight weeks pregnant. So, we heard that Langley was getting better and that Seaton was good. So, those were the determining things for us.*

If we are here, we should be supporting our neighborhood school. We will know at least half the kids in the classrooms.

At Langley, [diversity] is a huge part of the conversation. How are we including all of the parents in the discussion? The PTO is a lot of White women. So, what are the barriers to other people coming in?

I remember the first day of Black History Week two years ago, at Langley, they did a black hoodie day. And I was like, "This is awesome. What a fascinating place to live." That level of activism—that's a statement that the school didn't think twice about the fact of whether that would be acceptable to the parents. They're like: "Send your kids in a black hoodie to make this statement."

SUKI LUCIER. *Seaton is the most diverse elementary school in all of DCPS. It has diversity that if your core mission was diversity, you would have a hard time coming up with what has happened at Seaton completely organically. We have racial diversity, language diversity and there's also socioeconomic diversity.*

Encouraging diverse neighborhoods gets you to an organically diverse school. It's best when diversity happens organically.

Looking at Shaw, from U Street to Gallery Place, it's really one of the most diverse parts of D.C. Where the boundaries are drawn does make it a little bit interesting, because we draw from Chinatown, and we draw from some apartment buildings. Policy matters in creating affordable housing, creating dense housing, having a school in a walkable area. I think all of those things contributed.

With the whole school choice landscape in D.C., all of a sudden, the schools are commodities, and you're competing for customers, except it is kids and families.

School choice ends up being a weapon in the hands of White parents. If you give White parents a choice, they're going to choose to surround their kids with other White kids. The data bears it out; this is not an opinion. There's that perception that what is White must be the best.

I just constantly question if I'm the right person for the job and the best person for the job as the PTO president. As a White woman, should I even be in that position?

There's this kind of tug and pull because the diversity of the school was one of the things that attracted us to it. But of course, by coming to it and being part of it, there's some aspect of destroying the thing you love. I don't think I really considered what impact we would have coming into that diverse space as middle-class White people.

At the time, nobody wanted to do the job, and I stepped into it. So, I tell myself that, but there's still this thing of, because I stepped into that position, it meant that it wasn't there, open for somebody else. If I hadn't stepped into it, would there have been more space for people that might represent our community better?

When I was starting out as president, DCPS and Ward 6 Schools did this presentation about how to create community in diverse schools. I'm so, so thankful. They talked about how you have to be deliberate about it, that it doesn't just happen and that it might feel awkward to be explicit about the fact that you're trying to have a racially balanced board. It was really good to kind of rip that off and just be like, "Hey, we want to make sure that we represent our community."

They talked about the importance of creating opportunities for community to come together around free stuff—of trying to make things as accessible as possible.

With fundraising, if there are families who have money, and they would like to give money to us, why should we not take their money and create opportunities for them to give it to us?

But with money also brings a sense of entitlement and ownership. They're like, "I gave this money, why shouldn't I get that my kid that program?"

Where I've come down for the time being is that whatever monetary gain we might get from doing more fundraising events, we would lose it in the school camaraderie and the sense that we are inclusive.

It should never be pay-to-play to be part of the PTO, to be part of the school and to be part of the activities.

If we have an event, whether it's fundraising or anything else, I want every single family participating and at the same level—not where some people can afford to bid and some people can be the people that help with the event. I never wanted to get anywhere close to that.

I really tried to make sure that the majority of the time that we are holding events for the community that they're free.

Where we've landed on is a couple of different modes of fundraising: we have this gentrified neighborhood, and we have all these resources around us, so let's look out into our community more. And if we do have people that have more resources and more education and they are savvy around stuff like nonprofits and grant writing, awesome, let's use those people. So, we're getting more grants.

I wish that when people are on House Hunters *they would be like, "Well, that place had a great yard, but the neighborhood isn't diverse, and I don't want our kids going to a school just surrounded by kids who look like them." I wish people would value it more.*

I'm okay with my kid not going to as high-quality a school, whatever that means—to go to a school that's more diverse. My friend's kid somewhere else is playing the flute in third grade. We're never going to have that here.

My opinions on school choice and charter schools have changed so radically since becoming a parent.

It's made me, at a fundamental level, question this whole thing of "I just want what's best for my child," which feels like the ultimate parent privilege—to be able to look out for your kid. And I think a lot of us probably have said things like: "Well, of course I want my kid to be in a diverse school, but I'm not going to sacrifice my child on the altar of my educational ideals." I'm sure I've said that phrase myself. But maybe we should think about it. Maybe the kids like ours, with really wide margins, maybe we need to be okay with our kids having less than the best.

Every family has to do what's best for their kids. But maybe those of us in the positions of privilege need to rethink that.

I also think we've kind of been sold this lie that there's a solution to the racial problem where everybody benefits. We want it to be a win-win situation, where everybody comes out better than we are now. And I don't

Kennedy Recreation Center, 1950s. *Emil A. Press slide collection, D.C. History Center.*

think that's realistic—I don't. I think they have to give something. And that's scary. That's an investment. And that's radical.

You guys might have to take some steps back for other people to take steps forward. It's easier for me to say that when I'm not struggling financially, when I have steps to take back and still be safe. My margins are wide.

There are issues where you need to extend your cost-benefit analysis beyond your immediate family. I think it's something that we as White parents need to start thinking radically about, and even if, at the self-serving level, are we even best serving our children by doing that?

No, he doesn't need every advantage. He already has tons of them. I think we better serve them by having them in diverse environments.

8

CRIME, HOMELESSNESS AND COMMUNITY

You see the library destroyed, and you're thinking, "Gosh, people like that exist—hard to believe." And then you see it restored and repaired. And you wonder, "Do people like that exist? Hard to believe."
—Ruxandra Pond

These days, remnants of the drug trade exist, and the homeless population is present on the streets. According to crime data, violent crime has dropped over the last twenty years. In Ward 5, which includes Bloomingdale, LeDroit Park and a large portion of the northeast quadrant of Washington, D.C., there were 1,236 incidents of violent crime in 2000; by 2020, there were 676.[63]

As with other topics, the perception of crime and risk really varies based on who is looking; residents who lived through the decades of open-air drug markets and have seen the drug activity diminish may look at the one or two drug outposts differently than a newcomer. On the other end, someone who grew up in a peaceful suburb and is new to the neighborhood may be in proximity to drug dealing and homelessness for the first time in their lives.

Monthly neighborhood meetings, like Civic Association meetings and Area Neighborhood Commission (ANC) meetings, offer neighbors one of the most concrete opportunities to understand the reality of crime in their neighborhood. While perceptions differ among residents, the information shared at these meetings feels objective: a Metropolitan Police Department

Howard Drug Store at the corner of Seventh Street and Florida Avenue Northwest, 1950s. *Emil A. Press slide collection, D.C. History Center.*

(MPD) officer kicks off every meeting with data about crime activity over the preceding month and talks directly with concerned residents.

At one such meeting in early 2021, Captain Augustine of the MPD joined the ANC 6E meeting and launched into a rundown of the police-necessitating activity in March: a homicide near the Giant Supermarket, an uptick of robberies and car jackings and arrests at a local store that had found a niche selling goods along with a "gift" of marijuana (which is legal to own in small quantities in D.C. but illegal to sell).

Several residents expressed concern about the homicide; the area has seen constant gun violence over the last few years and a spike in 2020 and 2021. "This activity seems so predictable," said one resident who lives within sight of the area. "The crowd gathers, and within a few hours, I hear gunshots. I've witnessed far too many shootings. If it's predictable, it's preventable." "How do you reduce violence in that section of our neighborhood?" asked another. The captain sympathized with the residents but didn't offer any immediately comforting plans. "That area is nerve-wracking even for our officers," said Augustine. "Gunshots have gone off even when the officers are sitting right there. It's not easy to make arrests—a lot of surveillance needs to happen. But significant MPD assets have gone into that area, and arrests are happening."

Other topics touched on that night offered a snapshot of issues that niggle at those living in a gentrifying neighborhood; an unexpectedly hot topic was illegal dumping into public trash cans. The residents and commissioners spent thirty minutes circling the issue, trying to come up with a plan to discourage residents from illegally dumping such a large amount of private trash in public cans that the cans overflow. Options exist, they noted, like calling the city for bulk pickup. The annoyance about this behavior was palpable during the conversation, as commissioners proposed fines as high as $500 as punishment for those caught doing this.

Finally, the real source of the annoyance emerged: "This is happening in an area with million-dollar row houses," said a commissioner. "This is not a low-income thing. This is coming from residents who simply don't care. I can actually identify the people in my neighborhood who are doing it, and an impactful fine would make a difference."

SCOTT ROBERTS. *I created welcome baskets and some other stuff in the early 1990s. At first, I'd go to community meetings and it's like, "Here is the list of police officers who serve our neighborhood." So, you had the list of the officers and their telephone numbers. You had a list from the U.S. Department of Community Services and Supervision Agency—a federal agency that supervises parolees and probationers. There was a list of the parole and probation officers that served the neighborhood, and I would pass that out at community meetings. Can you imagine doing that today?*

I remember going to my first Civic Association meeting. There was a schism: one group was accused of stealing money. There was screaming and yelling. I was naive, I heard all these really nasty names that some of my Black neighbors were calling my other Black neighbors. I thought, "I'm just going to sit in the back of the room and not say anything. I'm not going to repeat these words; these are nasty words." That wasn't everybody, but it's like, "Oh, wow, I moved into a really interesting neighborhood. A colorful, animated discussion."

The kind of crimes that you saw at Logan Circle, they moved over here. Like people getting held up while unpacking their car in the daytime. That's the kind of stuff we didn't have here—it moved. So, the stuff you used to see in Logan Circle in the 1990s moved here—yay!

LEROY THORPE. *There ain't no drug situation now. There are no open-air drug markets around here, except a little bit of a residue at Seventh and S Streets, where I think you might have some type of heroin market or something. It's not like it used to be.*

Now, the problems are car break-ins, some minor burglary, particularly during the holiday season; people stealing packages—stuff like that.

Then you had K2 come in and kick in and synthetic drugs. It didn't cost a lot of money to get the same high, but the high was poisonous.

Greg Mason. *Just very recently, they had an issue right there in the liquor store parking lot with guys selling heroin. I mentioned something to the guy that runs the store. He knew it, but I think he was kind of scared.*

They were around there for a minute—a couple years. I got tired of it. Because the house that has the mural on the side of the wall, that's my buddy house, he's an African man, and his daughters are like my goddaughters.

And I said, "Naw, I'm tired of this." I made some phone calls. I got some friends on the police force, high up, that I know. And I told them. They said: "Don't worry, we'll take care of it." And when I saw the guy that owns the building, he told me, "Man, they're not around here no more."

Ruxandra Pond. *I had my child, and I was also watching my two little nephews; we were out on the field here before the renovations two and a half years ago. We were playing, and then there were some guys right here on V Street playing on ATVs or all-terrain vehicles. And they were being very loud, but whatever. But then, at some point, one guy went around and came in onto the park on his ATV and basically got up on the field. And I panicked because all the three kids were in different places on the field. And he came right at us. I just freaked out.*

It felt really threatening. And he played chicken. He literally drove up to us as fast as he could until the very last moment. And I was just trying really hard to grab and shield the kids and then he, you know, he laughed and kind of went off.

There are so many different people here; there are definitely tensions. But everything that we've done as Friends of the Park or as a community, we try to do in an effort to get to know each other, because the more you get to know each other, the less difficult it is to work things out.

We tried to bring out pizza to get to know the kids, for example. Some the kids who play in the park are, as all kids would be while unsupervised, unruly, and they damaged park property—as all kids would if they're not being closely watched. We thought, "Well, if we get to know them—if we know their names, and they know ours—maybe they'll listen to us."

There's been a lot of interactions where we say, "Please, don't throw rocks," or whatever.

That makes a whole load of difference. And I think that builds kind of a rapport, where they know that I'm in the park every day, and they won't get away with silliness.

I have to admit, I think it's very hard. I've had many times when I've gone home and been very upset that my kid was threatened or had rocks thrown at her or was scared by something, and we had to leave.

You know the free little library in the park? It's been hurt a few times. Recently, it was very severely damaged—the glass broke or the plastic broke off those doors. And then, overnight, someone fixed it and left a beautiful note—really just a heart-achingly beautiful note.

The typewritten note:

Dear neighbors,

We repaired this little free library with our own money and lack of woodworking skills because we love it so much and were sad to see it destroyed. Please take care of it and each other during these uncertain times.

"That is part of the beauty of all literature. You discover that your longings are universal longings, that you're not lonely and isolated from anyone. You belong."
—F. Scott Fitzgerald

"Words are, in my not-so-humble opinion, our most inexhaustible source of magic, capable of both inflicting injury and remedying it."
[—J.K. Rowling]

BLACK LIVES MATTER
love,
your strange neighbors

Note on Free Little Library, LeDroit Park. *Ruxandra Pond.*

133

RUXANDRA POND. *That was a micro example of everything that goes on in our park and our community. You know, there's vandalism, and there's also lots of love and community and random acts of kindness.*

You see the library destroyed, and you're thinking, "Gosh, people like that exist—hard to believe." And then you see it restored and repaired. And you wonder, "Do people like that exist? Hard to believe."

PREETHA IYENGAR. *But I do think that, recently, reading about the shootings has been really scary. Because its* [proximity to] *the playground aspect of it. But we didn't see it. No one has gotten hurt, but they could have. You could just be walking down the street, and something could randomly happen to you. That's the scary part about it. It's not about doing the "right thing" and you will be OK. You could just be minding your own business.*

The other thing that really scared me was when Tricia McCauley was murdered. [In 2016, McCauley was entering her car in Bloomingdale when a man forced his way into her car and raped and murdered her.][64] *And I know some people who are moving because of the stuff at the playgrounds. So, it is affecting people.*

But what bothers me more are the shootings and the gangs and because it is kids doing the shootings. They are kids. They are not thinking; they don't even understand what they are doing. That's not true—they can think but just act on their impulses. We all did it; it's just that I didn't have a gun, and I was in a very supported and structured environment and didn't have to worry about food and deal with all this other stuff.

But how do you do it in a way where you aren't just calling cops on people who aren't really doing anything? But if you do call the cops because there is a drug deal you are seeing but they don't see it, they can't do anything anyways. And you don't want to call the cops on someone who is just hanging out.

GRETCHEN WHARTON. *I don't know the answers to some of the larger drug and homeless problems; it's a huge, huge problem. I feel so bad for these young people who you know are addicted. I see so many homeless; I don't know if they are from shelters or if they are in homes for people with mental issues—every morning, I see five or six men come up this way. Every day.*

It was amazing; for a number of years after the gentrification happened, we had zero problems—none. Now, all of a sudden, people are saying to me, "Where are these people coming from?" In the last two years—once they closed St. Elizabeth's and started opening up homes.

Two or three of them stand out here and talk to themselves all the time. I don't know, but I'm sure it's got to be the follow-up to closing St. Elizabeth's. So, that part has changed. They don't seem violent. But every day now—and I haven't done this for so many years—I go out there and pick up pints of vodka bottles out of my yard. And that wasn't happening for a couple of years. So, that's something not-so-good that's happened.

I don't think anyone has a clue what to do about the homeless population. You can't just build a home; they need so many services, including mental health services.

Homelessness was another topic of discussion at the April 6, 2021 ANC meeting. Two sizable homeless encampments existed in Shaw. One public park was home to more than two dozen tents, and Seaton Elementary School had about twelve tents lined up next to the playground. Because the park was slated for a renovation, and school was slowly reopening after the 2020 shutdown, the commissioners were concerned that the unhoused people who were occupying those spaces would be uprooted and left to find another patch of earth.

For the commissioners and residents present at the meeting, the problem of homelessness was primarily a problem of finding homes for the unhoused. Some commissioners wanted to draft a resolution that encouraged Washington, D.C., to continue a program that was using funds from FEMA to put the homeless in hotels; other commissioners wondered if there was a way to allow them to occupy vacant apartments and houses. "We are looking for a win-win solution," said commissioner Michael Eichler at the meeting. "We need to improve the living conditions for the people experiencing homelessness, and we need to establish lines of communication so residents can be heard." "This is the number-one thing that I hear from constituents about," said another commissioner. "Homelessness is an issue that is facing every corner of the district."

The commissioners unanimously sought to encourage the mayor to find temporary housing for that community. "This resolution makes me happy to live in a community where the commissioners care about everyone who lives in the community, including the unhoused," said another commissioner. "It's nice to see that ANC 6E is looking to prevent the displacement of the unhoused."

However, a few weeks later, the encampments became a neighborhood flashpoint. One of the tent dwellers near Seaton Elementary was arrested with a firearm a few blocks away, and the police found more ammunition in his tent. When news of the arrest hit the neighborhood and school community, it was like an emergency alarm had sounded. The empathetic tone toward the homeless quickly shifted to one of a potential threat. "Concern for them and support for them should not come at the cost of the safety and security of our students," said Eichler to a reporter from WUSA9.[65] Parents and neighbors reacted in fear and fury, and the school listserv blew up with outrage. Some parents began a campaign to contact the mayor's office, the city councilmembers and the media to remove the encampment from its location so close to the elementary school.

The campaign worked. By May 7, 2021, the unhoused people had all been offered spots at shelters or in hotels, the tents had been broken down and the encampment was gone. By May 13, a fence blocked off the area.

PREETHA IYENGAR. *There was one situation where I did call authorities, and I'm not entirely sure if this was the right thing to do. When I walk to our daycare at Northwest Settlement House, I walk down Rhode Island Avenue, past the gas stations, and there are two blocks of that block that I really don't like walking because it is pedestrian hostile—no shade, lots of traffic and illogical crossings. In that bus stop, people were essentially living there; there were upholstered chairs and suitcases. It was dirty, and that sidewalk was so small, and I had to walk my kid by there every day. And there were people passed out on the corner from I don't know what. Whoever was getting drunk there was throwing the trash, and it was collecting around the trees. So, I called about that, and it started getting cleaned every week. It took me a month to get to someone. I had to be pretty persistent.*

And then, one day, the people were gone, and their stuff was gone, and part of me was like, "I'm glad I'm not walking through that anymore." But I also felt guilty. I don't actually know what happened to them, but sadly, I don't think it was anything more than their stuff getting taken away, forcing them to move.

The things that do bother me, because I walk up and down North Capitol Street to work, and you do see people passed out on the street, or there are homeless people walking into the traffic. That is scary. I also don't like being approached, especially near Big Ben Liquor. Right across the street there is a public housing building and a ton of people gathered there, but I didn't have a problem.

It would be nice to give homeless people a safe place to go. It is kind of sad—the homeless population here. This is the nation's capital, and this is the best we can do for people? Really, we can't do any better than shoveling away their tents?

Neighbors across race and economic statuses meet at neighborhood meetings, like the ANC meeting and Civic Association meetings. They can also interact online, on neighborhood-specific social media sites like NextDoor or on a Facebook group. How else can a community grow in a diverse environment?

GRETCHEN WHARTON. *I think you have to have common causes* [to build community].

For instance, I've rallied the people around to get our streets widened. The 400–500 block of S Street Northwest, you'll notice, the sidewalks are narrow. When I grew up, there were wider sidewalks; there were trees, and the streets were more narrow. When I was young, the federal government came in and took part of our yard, made the sidewalk smaller to widen the streets. Sixth Street was managed by federal highway, and they wanted to expedite the suburban government works out of D.C. They came North on Sixth Street Northwest, East on S Street Northwest, up Fourth Street Northwest. Finally, I've gotten DDOT to acknowledge this. I think in the next couple of years, we can get our sidewalks and trees back. That will slow down the traffic and make the sidewalks ADA compliant. In doing that, that has become a common neighborhood cause, and I've gotten a number of residents to rally behind.

MICHELLE CARTHEN. *I was on the board at Crispus Attucks Park.*

And I remember being on the park board, the first sign of the tension that I noticed is when, at the park, they were trying to decide on "kids or dogs." This was my first experience with, "Dogs? What? Y'all want to turn it into a dog park? I have boys. They play football; they have been playing football out there for many years, and you are not taking that away." We were trying to figure out how to create a dog play park. That was crazy.

I was livid. They're just dogs! One of my Black friends grew up in a White neighborhood. She helped me understand that in the White community, dogs are family.

[My neighbor John Corea] *somehow ended up just getting rid of the building and flattening the land out there. John was the one that led all of that.*

I don't even remember how I got on the board. I was probably out there volunteering to do something one day and thought, "I'd like to be a part of this." I stayed on the board for a long, long time.

We would be out there in the springtime, planting flowers and pulling weeds. In the wintertime, we would hang lights for Christmas trees. We organized a fundraiser every year, the yard sale. It was just a lot of fun, and John really brought a sense of community to the park and the neighbors who lived on the park.

At some point, something happened with the business registration; it didn't get refiled. In D.C., you have to refile it many times. So, it was a long battle over a technicality.

We all got together; we put money in to make sure that we were able to hire a lawyer to represent the park. And that was one of the times where the community came back together. You could see it; you could feel it. The meetings were standing room only. People were very interested in making sure that we saved the park.

At that point, it wasn't a Black/White thing. It was a: "I live in this neighborhood. I enjoy the park; the park is an extension of my backyard."

SCOTT ROBERTS. *AOL came out in the early 1990s. Before that, you would still go to community meetings, and they would have pieces of paper—before email addresses. One of the things I included in the new neighbor packets— and honestly, I can't believe I did this—was a list of the people who had been murdered in the neighborhood in the past couple of years.*

I did it. I honestly did it. Did I really do that? Can you imagine that today?

Then email came along; people are moving in who are all younger than me—people in their twenties and thirties. And I remember people saying, "What's your Twitter account?" And I said "What? OK, I have to do this. Let's do Twitter; let's do Facebook." And it just took off.

If I can toot my own horn, with the listserv, I control it, I manage it, I keep track of what's going on and if there's something that really needs to be addressed, other people can do it as well. If there's a crime issue, other people can Tweet to the police, contact their councilmember or mayor.

My perception of NextDoor is that there is no one really managing or controlling it—it just exists. There is no one who controls it, who cares what is there.

Nowadays, if someone is renovating and they have construction and they have construction workers parking in the alley, people go on NextDoor or Twitter to complain. Even in the aughts, if you saw someone renovating, it was like, "Oh! Someone is renovating—happy day! Let's have a party!" You go up and say: "What are you doing? This is great!" You are happy that someone is doing something.

Now, I went to a D.C. water meeting—we are having another D.C. Water project—and people were complaining about something that I considered really innocuous. Like, can't you just handle this yourself? This is not a real problem! So, they say, "When is the city coming to maintain the tree boxes? To do the weeding?"

It's like, "What? You think the city weeds the tree boxes? No—you do that!"

I have to make this observation. When I moved in in the 1990s, people who bought a house who weren't investors became community stakeholders. We all got involved in one way or another. We all worked out who was doing what. We all looked after stuff. If there were issues, we would call DCRA, call DPW, we would get involved.

Now we have full-house residences, half house residences, a small number of three-unit houses. My observation is that half-house condo owners and renters are not community stakeholders. They don't give a damn about the neighborhood at all. They don't get involved. They don't introduce themselves; they don't care. They are short-timers and to hell with everything going on in the neighborhood. How many half-house condo owners do you know who came up to you and introduced themselves? How many have stayed in touch with you? Can you count them on one hand?

Realtors love that, but that is the transition. You end up building a neighborhood with higher turnover, real estate wise, but people aren't necessarily invested in the neighborhood.

PREETHA IYENGAR. *We go to these meetings; we used to go to the Bloomingdale Civic Association, but to be honest, these meetings are at 7:00 p.m. We just gave up. We thought, "This is not ever happening for us." When we had one kid, sometimes, we could do it, but with two kids— if everybody has food and gets to a bed at some point, it's like, "Great!"*

So, we used to go to BCA meetings, especially after Tricia McCauley was murdered, and one of the moms organized something. She called this group together; I was trying to get data and a survey of families and organize people.

I was trying to get families to go to the meetings and be vocal. But I got very busy with the kids. We tried to meet with councilmember Kenyon McDuffie, but we are all young parents; it's very hard to get people to come out. It's difficult for everybody to do. We tried for a little bit, but it fell through the cracks.

9

INTEGRATION

How Stable Is It? Who Benefits? Who Is Hurt?

Let me ask you a question—you name one healthy integrated neighborhood. When you say, "Oh, the diversity!" The diversity is a code word for "White people are moving into Black neighborhoods."
—Leroy Thorpe

At the beginning of this book, Gretchen Wharton, Greg Mason and Michelle Carthen told us about growing up in a neighborhood that was largely Black.

Though the newest houses now hit the market at more-than-million-dollar prices, many residents have stayed in their homes and created a neighborhood with a notable amount of income and race diversity. Residents at every level of the economic ladder—lower income, middle class and wealthy—exist alongside each other. Black, White, Latino and Asian residents live, work and go to school alongside each other. Some residents carry decades of history about the neighborhood inside of them; others just know what they have seen in the few years they have lived here.

What does it feel like to live in an integrated neighborhood? Who benefits? And does everyone feel that they belong?

> GRETCHEN WHARTON. *As I reflected back, I thought it was never going to become what it is today without integration and gentrification.*

Florida Avenue Northwest in Shaw, 1950s. *Emil A. Press slide collection, D.C. History Center.*

Florida Avenue Northwest in Shaw, 2021. *Shilpi Malinowski.*

MICHELLE CARTHEN. *It doesn't feel like community anymore. It just feels like a place where we live. That's what it feels like.*

As I've watched the city change and I've listened to all sides of the story from my friends and family members, a lot of them were angry. They didn't like that the White people were moving in, and they were taking over.

I didn't really buy into that theory. My thought was, "Yep, they are moving in, they are adding resources, they're building up the neighborhood."

We don't have the money, we don't have the resources, we don't have the time.

JOHN LUCIER. *For a while, we were getting called "honky" or "cracker" every week. It has been so long since that's happened to us. I grew up in Ohio, and I freaked out when I was in Columbia Heights. I have always been a part of a majority-White community. But then I moved here.*

SUKI LUCIER. *I came in 2003, and people were very surprised that I was OK with it. There is a combination of factors that made me comfortable. I grew up in Long Island in the 1980s and went into the city with my parents. It was rough. My mom's a minister, and she worked in Flushing, Queens, and she found somebody stabbed to death in the vestibule one morning. So, my perception of what is an acceptable level of crime is probably skewed.*

I remember how shocking it was when we started seeing other White people in the neighborhood. I started seeing groups of White people and was like, "Oh! This is different." And then going down Rhode Island Avenue and North Capitol Street, seeing a group of White people at 10:00 p.m.—that was completely different.

JOHN LUCIER. *Seeing two twenty-five-year old White women walking around at 10:00 p.m.—that was totally different.*

SUKI LUCIER. *There were people in the neighborhood early on who looked at us warily, and now I look back and think, "Oh, you were right. We were the harbinger." I'm not saying it's bad or good, but it definitely changed the makeup.*

There is this core of people who have been on the block, and there is diversity on the block. That is nice. Butch, Lana, Sunny. For us, it's nice that that core group of people stayed; it makes it feel less—there are benefits, but it feels like the same neighborhood.

From my perspective, I think interactions are by and large respectful. We see a lot less of people sitting on their stoops. Places have gotten

Children playing in LeDroit Park, mid-1900s. *John P. Wymer photograph collection, D.C. History Center.*

Seaton Place Northwest in Bloomingdale, 2021. *Shilpi Malinowski.*

fixed up, they have central AC and people didn't grow up sitting on stoops. So, some of those interactions have been lost. But there have been other opportunities—sidewalk cafés, renovation of the Florida Avenue playground, the library.

I realized I don't think I've necessarily always done the right calculation. And I think it's a little more complicated with something that's really a Black space and that's held as culturally distinct? You can see, OK, maybe that's not a place for me. I don't need to kind of bring my Whiteness on in there. But then there's certainly more marginal places like public schools and other community organizations that are more open and that maybe are more of a mix.

Leroy Thorpe. *I feel that the White folks around here look at me like, "What are you doing here?" They don't know the history. They don't know I closed the crack houses down. I am saying to myself, "By me shutting down the crack houses and open-air drug markets, you're safe!" They benefited by my work.*

The new White people are not used to Black people. They are really not used to seeing Black people, are really not used to Black people doing well. They are used to what they see on TV—the stereotypes.

The White folks colonized this place, and Black people helped them do it. Black people contributed to it.

When their parents left them the house, they were on drugs or alcoholics, and they didn't keep up the taxes, so they watched the house go to White people. They try to sell the house, but they don't fix it up—they couldn't sell it. Some of them tried to take loans out and fix the houses, and they couldn't pay, or they didn't want to pay the loans.

One of our neighbors, she raised her kids in the house, and when she passed, they wouldn't pay the loan—they lost it. Or they are on drugs, lost the house. Or they sold it for cheap thinking they could get some money.

I'm going to tell you what happened to the Black community; I'm going to give it to you straight.

You can see that the Black population has decreased; there are fewer Black people because of gentrification—without a doubt.

It's definitely changed, it's changed for the worse in terms of the social aspect. White folks are coming in and colonizing this place. They are basically taking over. They are taking over. Most of the time, I see an agenda when White people come to a community. They want to control the politics, they want to control the economics, they want to control the education.

Gentrification is not good for this Black community because Blacks have nothing. There are no clubs—they took the clubs where Black people were going and replaced them with beer gardens for White people. They have places where Black kids would play on the grounds, and now, they are dog parks. So, you have a gentrified, segregated D.C. It's always been segregated. The White folks don't hang out with no Black people. Maybe in high society, when these people are the head of a company or a politician, but there is no socialization.

And Black people don't have nothing. But I told them that. The drug boys didn't trust each other to say, "Let's come together in business and buy the houses up and put Black people in them." They couldn't see the concept. They didn't trust each other, and they were looking at fast money, and they suffered. When I see them now, they say, "Oh, do you still live in Shaw?" "Yeah, I live in Shaw. I saved my money; I invested. The same advice I told you, I took my own advice." They are living out in Southeast, in Maryland, some in Virginia. Now, some are going to West Virginia.

I understand White folks very well. I was born and raised in Upstate New York; I'm from Dutchess County—still have a house there, matter of fact. So, I grew up there, I have a master's degree hanging up on the wall [in social work, from UDC]. *And I went to a White university and got a political science degree. I'm an educated man, so I try to help my people, but my people are very difficult to help because of the centuries of colonization and brainwashing and assimilation.*

Assimilation is no good. In order to make it in this country, you have to talk like a White person, act like a White person, then you are validated.

Me, I never went for that; I was never raised that way. I was half–West Indian; my grandfather came from Barbados, my grandmother from Haiti. My father was raised in Spanish Harlem, my mother in Florida, though she came up with the migration to the North, picking beans and what not, and finally met my father and married. I'm not a person who thinks that they need to be validated by another person or individual group or culture to be worth something. I know my individual worth, and what I'm concerned about is what my creator thinks. But Black people think I have to assimilate and act like them and talk like them—it's so disgusting for me to see something like that. Just be yourself.

GRETCHEN WHARTON. *I would like neighbors to be more friendly. I walk over and introduce myself to them, but it's not like it was. It was never going to be that way. Everyone is rushing and running and trying to take care of themselves, and the climate of the country has changed.*

I go to a lot of events now, and I'm on boards with people who live in Chevy Chase or Kalorama. I was telling one of my close White friends, "You know, there is still in D.C., there are still two separate worlds here. The decision making/power play role has always been at the behest of Caucasians. I want you to start looking at the parties you go to and come up with some observations."

And she called me back and said, "You are right. I've been to six parties in the last few months, and there were no people of color there."

I said, "These are the people influencing the key decisions here. There have always been two separate worlds."

It was so funny when she called me back and said: "You are right." I said, "I want you to be observant. I want you to be the observer in your social world."

It's always happened, and I was trying to tell her that it's still happening. The decisions are made on the golf course, on the tennis courts; they are approved in the boardroom. We never had a seat at the table, so we weren't part of that group.

It hasn't changed that much. And now in the era of Trump—I told someone, "The sheets were not thrown away; they were just taken off. Now, they are out again."

What Trump did is he brought them back out. They were never gone. They just feel that it's OK now to outwardly be racist.

LEROY THORPE. *Let me ask you a question—you name one healthy integrated neighborhood. When you say, "Oh, the diversity!" The diversity is a code word for "White people are moving into Black neighborhoods."*

Oh, it's diverse! It's diverse because White folks are coming in. When Black people try to move into White neighborhoods, White people move out. That's just the way the country is.

But [one White couple] are sweet, man. I wish all the gentrifying folks could be like them. They are very nice, respectful; we love them, my family and I love them. When a group of White people come into a historic Black community and gentrify, they should actually try to blend into the community. Every year, I throw a block party, in honor of the police department. They came to the block party and had a very good time. They came and blended in—that is the type of neighbors that we want, that want to be a part of the community. They are not coming in and trying to run something. They are beautiful human beings. Their parents raised both of them very well. There is no racism; there is no agenda there.

If I had more neighbors like them, then it would be lovely for Blacks and Whites to coexist. But usually, it's the White people who have the power, and they don't want to give it up or share it. They don't want to give it up; they want to keep you under them and to control you and you to be validated by them.

MICHELLE CARTHEN. *The boys were raised in this neighborhood, and my boys, especially the oldest one because he can remember the older neighborhood better than my younger son, he feels like, "Wow, I walk around in my neighborhood, and they look at me like I don't belong here. They don't understand that I was here first."*

GRETCHEN WHARTON. *The new residents don't do that* [say hello, look each other in the eye]. *First of all, they are young working people, they are ripping and running. In the summer, I have to grab the young ladies and say, "Take those earphones out! It's too dark, you don't know what's going on around you."*

And they kind of stay to themselves and don't interact. That makes it worse. Every time I see new people, I introduce myself because you know they are not going to introduce themselves. But once you do it, it's great! I introduced myself to a new renter over here, and she said, "OMG, you are the first person I've talked to!"

CHRISTINA PAPANICOLAOU. *We're trying, and there's more we can do. I mean, we're still settling in. It's only been two months and a half since we've lived here. But I think moving forward and living in this neighborhood, I do want to figure out a way we can be a part of the community even more and get to know people more.*

PREETHA IYENGAR. *I personally interact with everybody the same way—I try to in restaurants, I guess. I know there are Black families who have been here for a while, but going to parties at people's houses, that's not who we are seeing there. But it could also be that the parties are basically related to our kids. So, I don't think it's entirely intentionally. I'm not sure if I'm making something out of nothing.*

After I had my son, it took me a while to recover from the delivery. I remember I was walking down my block—my big block was to the end of the street—and there was a neighbor four or five doors down, and he's still there, and he was sitting on this porch. He saw me and he was like, "I know that walk." It was just really funny. He was like, "I've had five baby mamas. Are you OK?"

But when we go to Florida Avenue Playground, I wonder, "How can we share this, and how do we share this?" I don't know if it's just that after the farmers' market, one group is there, and at other times, other groups are there.

I love Halloween on Seaton Place. And that is everybody—all kids— it's very diverse. And teenagers, there is the whole gamut, they will show up at 10:00 p.m. But I love Halloween on this street because of that.

I'm really happy that my kid grows up thinking that all this stuff is normal. There's a gay couple, a lesbian couple, all kinds of mixed-race couples of every variety. You are proud of the diversity you have and where your family is from and the languages you can speak. In D.C., that's cool; you're cooler when you're bilingual. Everybody has a family abroad, as opposed to when we grew up, we were trying to assimilate. We had to explain to people the dots on my mom's forehead and what being vegetarian was. Versus here, it's almost like you are really celebrated for your cultural differences.

JOHN LUCIER. *The millionaires are still the minority, so I'm not even sure who they are.*

SUKI LUCIER. *I don't know if maybe they are newer, they haven't had kids yet, so they aren't as enmeshed in the neighborhood.*

I feel like I see more entitlement behaviors, like people leaving trash cans in ways that block other people, expired tags on cars.

GRETCHEN WHARTON. *I hate that sense of entitlement. If you are going to come into a neighborhood and be a neighbor, you have to work together.*

When you've lived here a long time, it's not just the obvious that you see changing, not just the buildings, it's the people, it's the social climate, it's that kind of thing, too. And you have to put it all together.

I saw a couple this morning walk down S Street, and one of my neighbor's houses doesn't have a fence. And they let the dog go in the yard and poop right by the steps. Why would you think it's alright to do that?

I love pets. I've had pets all my life, but you never let your dog poop without picking it up! The building right across from me is an apartment building that is not fenced in, and people think it's a dog park.

Help me understand why you think this is OK. That has nothing to do with color, I don't think. I just can't figure out that mindset. But it does have to do with being young and feeling entitled and privileged.

NICK GRUBE. *I think a lot about Hawaii when I lived there, where there's a real stark divide between locals and transplants, "Are you from here or not?" It's about this idea of being respectful of the place that you live.*

The term they use in Hawaii is "fucking haole." Don't be a "fucking haole." Haole is not necessarily a bad word. It means, generally, a White person who is not from the island. So, you can be haole, which is just describing somebody as White. I would be a haole kid, and it wouldn't be offensive. It just means I'm White and not from there.

But if somebody ever called me a fucking haole, that means you are being a disrespectful prick. You know, you're that drunk person running down the beach and not paying attention to the other people around you. You are trying to touch a sea turtle. It's just being oblivious.

You're using the place rather than being a part of it. You're extracting.

I think that always helps me when I think of navigating a new place. I've done it my whole life. I'm a military brat. I'm a journalist. I move around a lot. Just be respectful. Be nice. Say hello. Don't be a dick.

Howard Theater, 2021. *Shilpi Malinowski.*

I don't think that you would necessarily see that behavior happening that often if people lived in this neighborhood their whole lives. They probably would have gotten yelled at by, you know, somebody's mom or dad. They just know: don't piss off Mrs. Whoever down the street.

Suki Lucier. *White supremacy is still there and rotting away. What I think makes me hopeful is that conversations are happening more out in the open, the "sunshine is best antiseptic" thing. The fact that we're having more explicit conversations about this is good.*

I think White people need to do more examination. We shouldn't always assume that our presence in the space is going to be positive. And I think that's something that we're probably pretty guilty of as a group—or at least not contemplating the ways that we might have negative effects. We see ourselves as neutral, and that might not always be the case.

If you come from one environment and you go to the other, it can feel very confusing and uncomfortable. In some ways, with White privilege, we have an opportunity, if we want to, to go have a life that never makes us uncomfortable. It is possible for us to live a life where we never have to examine our race or our role. We can live that life, and we almost have to make a deliberate choice not to.

We've got to live together and educate our kids together and eat together. It's why living in D.C. has been so huge for me. Your neighbors are all sorts of different things.

Gus's school has really been an interesting part of what I think was my racial journey in the city. When he was in Pre-K-3 at a public charter school, he was very much in the minority in that school. He was one of two White kids in his class.

That was one of the first times for me of looking around in an auditorium and being like, "Oh, I'm the only White person here," and then having some of the feelings associated with that. Feeling like people might be looking at you or that they're going to judge other people of your race by your actions. It was just a very new and interesting situation, and it made me realize the importance of, like, living together and sending our kids to school together.

One of the big things that comes in with prejudice and everything else is viewing others as this monolithic other. All Black people do this, all Asian people do this, all White people do this. And then you get to know enough Black or Asian or White people, and you're like, "Oh, man, there are as many kinds of you as there are of me!"

LEROY THORPE. *Right now, you have the Black people who are doing well here and consumed with assimilation. They want to assimilate so they can feel a part of the community. So, they assimilate and support whatever the gentrifier people want to do.*

People like myself who have independent thinking prefer to not be a part of that. I don't think it's a fair and just thing to provide opportunities for just one segment of our society based on race and class and education.

I also blame the Black politicians. They did not train the younger Black people to come up and take their place; they wanted to hold on to their power. White people train; I saw it. Professors would take the White kids, have a beer with them at the café—I watched that interaction. Black people don't do stuff like that; they don't try to interact and try to train because they are selfish. They are scared they are going to lose something. There is jealousy and envy.

I try to help Black people all the time. I always try to pass knowledge down. I see the kids today, out there cursing. I say: "Your kid is out there cursing; he is acting juvenile. I don't want to deal with that. I'm trying to raise my daughter. They've got him, they are going to lead him down to a place you are going to have a hard time getting him back."

White folks have the city now because Black folks gave it to them. Black people had the city, and they let it go.

My thing is the only difference between me and you—or me and a White man—is our deeds. Who did the best deeds, who is doing the most good. Other than that, he's no better than me, and I'm no better than him other than what good you do. That's how I look at it.

When I step out here, I'm going to speak my mind. I don't have to beg. I have a skill; I'm gainfully employed. I know how to generate capital. My house is just about paid off. I think I have invested my money very well. When I step out here, I'm stepping out here confident.

MICHELLE CARTHEN. *I'm glad I stayed. I really am glad I stayed.*

GRETCHEN WHARTON. *There are a few people around here who say to me, "How can you say integration is positive?" And I say: "How can you think it's not?" We never would have had the money—the infrastructure money and development money—put in this neighborhood had it been an all-Black neighborhood, be real. That is just a reality.*

Community is what makes you feel good about where you live and what makes you want to stay there and make it grow. I spend my weeks on boards—the D.C. Commission on the Arts and Humanities and Shaw Main Streets.

"Art All Night" started here in Shaw, and then I took it to the D.C. Commission on the Arts and Humanities and said: "You really need to expand this." The initial idea was from Europe's Art Nuit Blanche. The whole idea for "Art All Night" is to have people out all night.

We want everybody out in the streets. This last year [2019], at parcel 42 at Seventh Street and Rhode Island Avenue [an undeveloped plot of land], we set up a site where people were there selling their art, and we had a stage there. At 2 and 3 o'clock in the morning, walking up Seventh Street, I couldn't get through the sidewalks; it was packed.

When I walk around here now, I think, "My goodness, I couldn't do this so many years ago!"

I do it a lot now; I walk up and down to see what's new and what's different now. Maybe in the last ten to fifteen years, I've started seeing people walking on the streets and feeling safe. It's amazing.

NOTES

Preface

1. Szekely, "Downtown LA."

Introduction

2. Rothstein, *Color of Law*.
3. Mock, "What It Will Take."
4. Glover, "Black California Couple Lowballed."
5. Kamin, "Black Homeowners."
6. Schneider, "Taking Stock."

Chapter 1

7. Asch and Musgrove, *Chocolate City*.
8. Ibid.
9. Ibid.
10. Ibid.
11. United States Census Bureau, "Data."
12. U.S. Bureau of Labor Statistics, "Inflation Calculator."
13. United States Census Bureau, "Data."

Chapter 2

14. Walker, *D.C. Riots*.
15. Ibid.
16. United States Census Bureau, "Data."
17. Corea, "Crispus Attucks Park."
18. Taylor, "Hats Off."
19. Barnes, "Shaw Neighbors Honor."

Chapter 3

20. LaFraniere, "Barry Arrest."
21. Asch and Musgrove, *Chocolate City*, 386.
22. Ibid., 395.
23. Cox, "Metro First Arrived."
24. Roberts, *Bloomingdale*.
25. D.C. Housing Finance Agency, "Finances the Redevelopment."
26. Metropolitan Police Department, "Ramsey."
27. National Police Foundation, "Community Policing."
28. Taylor, "Hats Off."

Chapter 4

29. Milloy, "Anthony Williams."
30. Executive Office of the Mayor, "Press Release."
31. Milloy, "Anthony Williams."
32. Asch and Musgrove, *Chocolate City*.
33. Zillow, "Home Values."
34. U.S. Bureau of Labor Statistics, "Calculator."
35. New Community Church, "History."
36. Castaneda, *S Street Rising*.
37. MANNA Homes for All.
38. DC.gov, "DC Department of Housing and Community Development."
39. Ibid.
40. Corea, "Crispus Attucks Park."
41. DePillis, "Bear Necessities."
42. DePillis, "ANC 5C Votes."

43. Ibid.
44. Williams, "D.C. Photographer."

Chapter 5

45. United States Census Bureau, "Data."
46. Turner, "Home Price Watch."
47. Wellborn, "Bloomingdale Housing Market."
48. Austermuhle, "D.C. Files Suit."
49. Austermuhle, "For the Developer."
50. Ibid.
51. Austermuhle, "D.C. Files Suit."
52. Shapira, "Couple Who Renovated."
53. JBG Smith.
54. Krouse, "JBG Buys."
55. Malinowski, "Wave of Modernist Condos."
56. DC.gov, "DC Department of Housing and Community Development."
57. Redfin, "317 R Street NW #2."
58. Hermann, "Woman Robbed."

Chapter 6

59. Redfin, "20001 Homes for Sale."
60. Schaul, Keating and Orton, "D.C. Region's 2018 Housing Market."

Chapter 7

61. DCPS, "Seaton Elementary School."
62. My School DC. "Seaton Elementary School."

Chapter 8

63. Urban Institute, "Our Changing City."
64. Alexander, "Man Sentenced."
65. Torres, "Parents, Neighbors Concerned."

BIBLIOGRAPHY

Alexander, Keith L. "Man Sentenced to 30 Years in Christmas Day Rape, Murder of D.C. Actress." *Washington Post*, November 17, 2017.

Asch, Chris Myers, and George Derek Musgrove. *Chocolate City: A History of Race and Democracy in the Nation's Capital.* Chapel Hill: University of North Carolina Press, 2017.

Austermuhle, Martin. "D.C. Files Suit Against Virginia Couple Over Shoddy House Renovations." WAMU 88.5, May 7. 2015.

———. "For the Developer from Great Falls, a Great Fall." WAMU 88.5, May 6, 2015.

Barnes, Denise. "Shaw Neighbors Honor Samaritan—Say Patrols Helped Reduce Crime." *Washington Times*, July 10, 2005, A09.

Castaneda, Ruben. *S Street Rising.* New York: Bloomsbury, 2014.

Corea, John. "Crispus Attucks Park History." www.crispusattucksparkdc.org.

Cox, Alex. "When the Metro First Arrived in Shaw and Columbia Heights, They Were Far Different Than They Are Today." *Greater Greater Washington*, September 20, 2016.

DC.gov. "D.C. Department of Housing and Community Development Tenant Opportunity to Purchase Assistance." www.dhcd.dc.gov.

———. "Home Purchase Assistance Program." www.dhcd.dc.gov.

———. "Inclusionary Zoning Affordable Housing Program DC DHCD." www.dhcd.dc.gov.

D.C. Housing Finance Agency. "DCHFA Finances the Redevelopment of Sursum Corda in NoMa." December 15, 2020. www.globenewswire.com.

DCPS. "Seaton Elementary School." www.profiles.dcps.dc.gov.

Depillis, Lydia. "ANC 5C Votes Against Big Bear Cafe Liquor License." *Washington City Paper*, July 21, 2010.

———. "Bear Necessities: Will Booze Fuel Bloomingdale's Renaissance or Regression?" *Washington City Paper*, May 27, 2010.

Executive Office of the Mayor. "Press Release: Mayor Highlights 2004 Accomplishments." *DC Watch*, December 15, 2004. www.dcwatch.com.

Glover, Julian. "Black California Couple Lowballed by $500k in Home Appraisal, Believe Race was a Factor." *ABC News*, February 12, 2021.

Hermann, Martin Weil, and Peter Hermann. "Woman and Child Critically Wounded in Shooting Near Shaw and Logan Circle, D.C. Police Say." *Washington Post*, May 18, 2021.

Hermann, Peter. "Woman Robbed at Gunpoint While Unloading Car in Front of Her 2-Year-Old." *Washington Post*, May 26, 2016.

JBG Smith. www.jbgsmith.com.

Kamin, Debra. "Black Homeowners Face Discrimination in Appraisals." *New York Times*, August 25, 2020.

Krouse, Sarah. "JBG Buys Metro's Florida Ave. Sites for $10.2M." *Washington Business Journal*, July 11, 2011.

LaFraniere, Sharon. "Barry Arrest on Cocaine Charges in Undercover FBI, Police Operation." *Washington Post*, January 19, 1990.

Malinowski, Shilpi. "Wave of Modernist Condos Ushers in New Age of D.C. Architecture." *Washington Post*, June 1, 2017.

MANNA Homes for All. www.mannahoc.org.

Metropolitan Police Department. "Charles H. Ramsey." www.mpdc.dc.gov.

Milloy, Cortland. "Anthony Williams Is Credited with Helping to Revitalize D.C. Now He's Working to Make Sure Everyone Benefits." *Washington Post*, December 17, 2017.

Mock, Brentin. "What It Will Take to Close the Race Gap in Home Appraisals." Bloomberg CityLab, March 3, 2021.

My School DC. "Seaton Elementary School." www.myschooldc.org.

National Police Foundation. "Community Policing." www.policefoundation.org.

New Community Church. "New Community Church History." www.newcommunitychurchdc.org.

Redfin. "317 R Street NW #2." www.redfin.com.

———. "20001 Homes for Sale." www.redfin.com.

Roberts, Scott. *Bloomingdale: A Blog for the Bloomingdale Neighborhood*. www.bloomingdaleneighborhood.blogspot.com.

Rothstein, Richard. *The Color of Law: A Forgotten History of How Our Government Segregated America.* New York: Liveright, 2017.

Schaul, Kevin, Dan Keating and Kathy Orton. "The D.C. Region's 2018 Housing Market, Mapped." *Washington Post*, March 27, 2019.

Schneider, Jay W. "Taking Stock." *Valuation*, December 1, 2020, 12–17.

Shapira, Ian. "Couple Who Renovated D.C. Rowhouses Agree to Pay $1.3 Million to Fix Shoddy Work." *Washington Post*, June 7, 2016.

Szekely, Balazs. "Downtown LA's 90014 Heads the List of Fastest-Gentrifying ZIPs Since the Turn of the Millennium." RENTCafe, February 26, 2018. www.rentcafe.com.

Taylor, Guy. "Hats Off to a Safer Neighborhood—Residents Crack Down on Drugs." *Washington Times*, July 18, 2004, A09.

Torres, Matthew. "Parents, Neighbors Concerned Over Growing Homeless Encampment Next to Elementary School." WUSA9, April 21, 2021.

Turner, Lark. "Home Price Watch: Prices Rise 20% in Bloomingdale." UrbanTurf, April 21, 2014.

United States Census Bureau. "Explore Census Data." www.data.census.gov.

Urban Institute. "Our Changing City: Public Safety." www.apps.urban.org.

U.S. Bureau of Labor Statistics. "CPI Inflation Calculator." www.bls.gov.

Walker, J. Samuel. *The Washington, D.C. Riots of 1986: Most of 14th Street Is Gone.* New York: Oxford University Press, 2018.

Wellborn, Mark. "The Bloomingdale Housing Market, By the Numbers." UrbanTurf, September 16, 2020.

Williams, Elliot C. "This D.C. Photographer Captured 'The Last of Chocolate City' in Powerful Black-and-White Vignettes." DCist, December 9, 2019. AUTHOR: this source appears to be incomplete.

Williamson, Vanessa, Jackson Gode and Hao Sun. "We All Want What's Best for Our Kids." Think tank study, Brookings Institution, Washington, D.C.

Zillow. "Zillow Home Values." www.zillow.com.

ABOUT THE AUTHOR

 Shilpi Malinowski is a reporter whose work has been published in the *Washington Post*, the *New York Times* and *India Abroad*. For the past two decades, she has been reporting on life in neighborhoods in Washington, D.C., and within the Indian American diaspora. With a background in anthropology, she investigates how people forge their identities and feel a sense of belonging as communities change around them. She lives in Shaw with her husband and two young sons and can often be found on neighborhood playgrounds. This is her first book.

CPSIA information can be obtained
at www.ICGtesting.com
Printed in the USA
BVHW022026051222
653490BV00002B/15